LEGAL RESEARCH EXERCISES

Following The Bluebook:
A Uniform System of Citation

Ninth Edition

By

Nancy P. Johnson

Law Librarian and Professor of Law
Georgia State University
College of Law Library

Susan T. Phillips

Director of the Law Library and Professor of Law
Texas Wesleyan University
School of Law Library

To Accompany

Berring & Edinger's

FINDING THE LAW

Mat #40346309

© West, a Thomson business, 2003
© 2005 Thomson/West
        610 Opperman Drive
        P.O. Box 64526
        St. Paul, MN 55164–0526
        1–800–328–9352
Printed in the United States of America

ISBN 0–314–15952–5

 TEXT IS PRINTED ON 10% POST CONSUMER RECYCLED PAPER

TABLE OF CONTENTS

Student's Introduction

Assignment:

STUDENT'S INTRODUCTION

Mastering efficient research skills is more important than ever in the current legal environment. This ninth edition of *Legal Research Exercises, Following The Bluebook: A Uniform System of Citation* will help you learn to master efficient legal research skills. In completing the assignments in this book, you should become familiar with many kinds of research materials and you can use this familiarity to formulate basic research strategy. You will develop skills in using your law library and you will feel more comfortable with legal citation format.

We intend that none of the questions in this book to be extremely time-consuming. If you cannot find an answer, ask your instructor for help. Read the relevant material in your legal research text before attempting to complete the assignments. When we ask for a full citation, we want you to include the case name, reporter citation, court (if necessary) and a year in your citation, as specified by the revised *The Bluebook: A Uniform System of Citation* (18th ed.).

Each assignment contains four variations (A, B, C, D). Since the questions are identical for the four variations, you will work on one variation.

Practice professionalism by reshelving your books once you answer the questions. It takes only a few seconds to reshelve the materials.

To supplement your in-class instruction and the materials in this legal research exercise book, you may want to review the CALI lessons on legal writing and legal research. You can find these lessons at http://www.CALI.org.

We have tried very hard to eliminate all errors, but we apologize for any that you may discover. We have learned that no matter how painstaking our efforts are in this regard, because of the republishing of legal materials, errors creep into a book of this nature as time passes. Please contact your instructors when you discover a problem.

Nancy P. Johnson
Georgia State University
College of Law Library
njohnson@gsu.edu

Susan T. Phillips
Texas Wesleyan University
School of Law Library
sphillips@law.txwes.edu

ASSIGNMENT ONE
FINDING AND CITING CASES
EXERCISE A

GOALS OF THIS ASSIGNMENT:
To teach you how to find cases when you have citations.
To acquaint you with the location of reporters in your law library.
To familiarize you with the rules for citing cases in *The Bluebook: A Uniform System of Citation*, **18th ed.**

CITATION RULES: Read the *Introduction*, Bluepages B1, Bluepages B5.1-B5.1.3, Rules 6.1, 10.2.1, 10.2.2, 10.3.1, 10.3.2, 10.4, 10.5 and refer to tables BT.2, T.1, T.6, and T.10 of *The Bluebook*. Apply these rules as you learn the correct citation for each case.
Throughout this book, when we ask that you provide a full citation, give the name, citation and date of the case, and any other necessary information (such as court) required by *The Bluebook*.

The first two questions introduce you to the rules for citing U.S. Supreme Court cases.
Example: *Loving v. Virginia*, **388 U.S. 1 (1967).**

United States Reports, abbreviated U.S. in case citation, is the official reporter. Note that no parallel, unofficial reporters are listed for U.S. Supreme Court cases when a U.S. citation is available. At the beginning of table T.1 in *The Bluebook*, read the instructions for the **Supreme Court.**

1.   If an opinion of the U.S. Supreme Court has not yet been published in *United States Reports*, which unofficial reporters should you cite instead, in order of preference?

2.   State the full citation for 533 U.S. 606.

The third question requires you to find and cite a U.S. Supreme Court case from before 1875. They published these cases in reporters known as **nominative** reporters, because they were generally known by the name of the person who compiled the volume. The form of citation for a case in a nominative reporter differs from the form for a case appearing in contemporary sources. Study the rules for citing cases found in nominative reporters (*The Bluebook* calls them "early American reporters." See Rule 10.3.2.). Here is an example of how to cite a U.S. Supreme Court nominative reporter: *Hughes v. Union Ins. Co.*, **21 U.S. (8 Wheat.) 294 (1823).**

3.   State the full citation for 17 U.S. 122. Note: For the date, use the year of the Court Term.

Next, you must find and cite a federal court of appeals case from a circuit. When citing a court of appeals case always list the circuit within the parentheses, along with the date. **Example:** ***Bonilla v. Volvo Car Corp.*****, 150 F.3d 62 (1st Cir. 1998).**

4.   State the full citation for 336 F.3d 601.

Now, find and cite a federal district court case. When citing a case from district court, the particular court is included within the parentheses. **Example:** ***Hillard v. Guidant Corp.*****, 76 F. Supp. 2d 566 (M.D. Pa. 1999).**

5.   State the full citation for 277 F. Supp. 2d 622. Note: The district is listed before the state--the division, if listed, is listed after. Always include the district in the citation, never the division.

In general, for state decisions the state and the name of the court should be included within the parentheses. However, do not include the name of the court if the court of decision is the highest court of the state. Here is an example of how to cite a Pennsylvania Supreme Court case. How do you know what to include in the parentheses? Read Rule 10.4(b) and look at the listing for Pennsylvania in table T.1. **Example:** ***Commonwealth v. Brayboy*****, 246 A.2d 675 (Pa. 1968).**

Find 859 A.2d 26 to answer Questions 6 and 7.

6.   State the full citation for 859 A.2d 26.

Should you ever cite the official version of a case? Yes, if the case is very old and there is no regional citation. Otherwise, you should cite it **only** if you are **including it in a document submitted to a state court whose local rules require citation to the official reporter.** (See Rule 10.3.1(a), Bluepages B5.1.3, and table BT.2.) Here is our previous example cited in such a context. **Example:** *Commonwealth v. Brayboy,* **431 Pa. 365, 246 A.2d 675 (1968).** Note: We followed Rule 10.4(b) and omitted the jurisdiction Pa. from the parentheses because it is unambiguously conveyed by the reporter title.

7. State the full citation for 859 A.2d 26, assuming you are including this citation in a document submitted to a Connecticut state court whose local rules require citing to the official report volume.

Next, find an opinion from a state intermediate appellate court and cite it correctly. **Example:** *Maluszewski v. Allstate Ins. Co.*, **640 A.2d 129 (Conn. App. Ct. 1994).**

Find 147 S.W.3d 697 to answer Questions 8 and 9.

8. State the full citation for 147 S.W.3d 697.

Our previous example of an intermediate state appellate court citation cited in a document submitted to a Connecticut state court whose local rules require citing to the official report volume would look like this. **Example:** *Maluszewski v. Allstate Ins. Co.*, **34 Conn. App. 27, 640 A.2d 129 (1994).**

9. State the full citation for 147 S.W.3d 697, assuming you are including this citation in a document to an Arkansas state court whose local rules require citing to the official report volume.

ASSIGNMENT ONE
FINDING AND CITING CASES
EXERCISE B

GOALS OF THIS ASSIGNMENT:
To teach you how to find cases when you have citations.
To acquaint you with the location of reporters in your law library.
To familiarize you with the rules for citing cases in _The Bluebook: A Uniform System of Citation_, 18th ed.

CITATION RULES: Read the _Introduction_, Bluepages B1, Bluepages B5.1- B5.1.3, Rules 6.1, 10.2.1, 10.2.2, 10.3.1, 10.3.2, 10.4, 10.5 and refer to tables BT.2, T.1, T.6, and T.10 of _The Bluebook_. Apply these rules as you learn the correct citation for each case.
Throughout this book, when we ask that you provide a full citation, give the name, citation and date of the case, and any other necessary information (such as court) required by _The Bluebook_.

The first two questions introduce you to the rules for citing U.S. Supreme Court cases. **Example: _Loving v. Virginia,_ 388 U.S. 1 (1967).**

United States Reports, abbreviated U.S. in case citation, is the official reporter. Note that no parallel, unofficial reporters are listed for U.S. Supreme Court cases when a U.S. citation is available. At the beginning of table T.1 in _The Bluebook_, read the instructions for the **Supreme Court**.

1.   If an opinion of the U.S. Supreme Court has not yet been published in _United States Reports_, which unofficial reporters should you cite instead, in order of preference?

2.   State the full citation for 534 U.S. 19.

The third question requires you to find and cite a U.S. Supreme Court case from before 1875. They published these cases in reporters known as **nominative** reporters, because they were generally known by the name of the person who compiled the volume. The form of citation for a case in a nominative reporter differs from the form for a case appearing in contemporary sources. Study the rules for citing cases found in nominative reporters (_The Bluebook_ calls them "early American reporters." See Rule 10.3.2.). Here is an example of how to cite a U.S. Supreme Court nominative reporter: **_Hughes v. Union Ins. Co.,_ 21 U.S. (8 Wheat.) 294 (1823).**

3.   State the full citation for 34 U.S. 607. Note: For the date, use the year of the Court Term.

Next, you must find and cite a federal court of appeals case from a circuit. When citing a court of appeals case always list the circuit within the parentheses, along with the date. **Example: *Bonilla v. Volvo Car Corp.*, 150 F.3d 62 (1st Cir. 1998).**

4.   State the full citation for 344 F.3d 1057.

Now, find and cite a federal district court case. When citing a case from district court, the particular court is included within the parentheses. **Example: *Hillard v. Guidant Corp.*, 76 F. Supp. 2d 566 (M.D. Pa. 1999).**

5.   State the full citation for 288 F. Supp. 2d 127. Note: The district is listed before the state—the division, if listed, is listed after. Always include the district in the citation, never the division.

In general, for state decisions the state and the name of the court should be included within the parentheses. However, do not include the name of the court if the court of decision is the highest court of the state. Here is an example of how to cite a Pennsylvania Supreme Court case. How do you know what to include in the parentheses? Read Rule 10.4(b) and look at the listing for Pennsylvania in table T.1. **Example: *Commonwealth v. Brayboy*, 246 A.2d 675 (Pa. 1968).**

Find 602 S.E.2d 534 to answer Questions 6 and 7.

6.   State the full citation for 602 S.E.2d 534.

Should you ever cite the official version of a case? Yes, if the case is very old and there is no regional citation. Otherwise, you should cite it **only** if you are **including it in a document submitted to a state court whose local rules require citation to the official reporter.** (See Rule 10.3.1(a), Bluepages B5.1.3, and table BT.2.) Here is our previous example cited in such a context. **Example:** *Commonwealth v. Brayboy,* **431 Pa. 365, 246 A.2d 675 (1968).** Note: We followed Rule 10.4(b) and omitted the jurisdiction Pa. from the parentheses because it is unambiguously conveyed by the reporter title.

7. State the full citation for 602 S.E.2d 534, assuming you are including this citation in a document submitted to a West Virginia state court whose local rules require citing to the official report volume.

Next, find an opinion from a state intermediate appellate court and cite it correctly. **Example:** *Maluszewski v. Allstate Ins. Co.,* **640 A.2d 129 (Conn. App. Ct. 1994).**

Find 688 N.W.2d 365 to answer Questions 8 and 9.

8. State the full citation for 688 N.W.2d 365.

Our previous example of an intermediate state appellate court citation cited in a document submitted to a Connecticut state court whose local rules require citing to the official report volume would look like this. **Example:** *Maluszewski v. Allstate Ins. Co.,* **34 Conn. App. 27, 640 A.2d 129 (1994).**

9. State the full citation for 688 N.W.2d 365, assuming you are including this citation in a document to a Nebraska state court whose local rules require citing to the official report volume.

7

8

ASSIGNMENT ONE
FINDING AND CITING CASES
EXERCISE C

GOALS OF THIS ASSIGNMENT:
To teach you how to find cases when you have citations.
To acquaint you with the location of reporters in your law library.
To familiarize you with the rules for citing cases in *The Bluebook: A Uniform System of Citation*, 18th ed.

CITATION RULES: Read the *Introduction*, Bluepages B1, Bluepages B5.1- B5.1.3, Rules 6.1, 10.2.1, 10.2.2, 10.3.1, 10.3.2, 10.4, 10.5 and refer to tables BT.2, T.1, T.6, and T.10 of *The Bluebook*. Apply these rules as you learn the correct citation for each case.
Throughout this book, when we ask that you provide a full citation, give the name, citation and date of the case, and any other necessary information (such as court) required by *The Bluebook*.

The first two questions introduce you to the rules for citing U.S. Supreme Court cases. **Example: *Loving v. Virginia*, 388 U.S. 1 (1967).**

United States Reports, abbreviated U.S. in case citation, is the official reporter. Note that no parallel, unofficial reporters are listed for U.S. Supreme Court cases when a U.S. citation is available. At the beginning of table T.1 in *The Bluebook*, read the instructions for the **Supreme Court**.

1.   If an opinion of the U.S. Supreme Court has not yet been published in *United States Reports*, which unofficial reporters should you cite instead, in order of preference?

2.   State the full citation for 535 U.S. 55.

The third question requires you to find and cite a U.S. Supreme Court case from before 1875. They published these cases in reporters known as **nominative** reporters, because they were generally known by the name of the person who compiled the volume. The form of citation for a case in a nominative reporter differs from the form for a case appearing in contemporary sources. Study the rules for citing cases found in nominative reporters (*The Bluebook* calls them "early American reporters." See Rule 10.3.2.). Here is an example of how to cite a U.S. Supreme Court nominative reporter: ***Hughes v. Union Ins. Co.*, 21 U.S. (8 Wheat.) 294 (1823).**

3.   State the full citation for 72 U.S. 62. Note: For the date, use the year of the Court Term.

Next, you must find and cite a federal court of appeals case from a circuit. When citing a court of appeals case always list the circuit within the parentheses, along with the date. **Example: *Bonilla v. Volvo Car Corp.*, 150 F.3d 62 (1st Cir. 1998).**

4.   State the full citation for 353 F.3d 528.

Now, find and cite a federal district court case. When citing a case from district court, the particular court is included within the parentheses. **Example: *Hillard v. Guidant Corp.*, 76 F. Supp. 2d 566 (M.D. Pa. 1999).**

5.   State the full citation for 298 F. Supp. 2d 1222. Note: The district is listed before the state—the division, if listed, is listed after. Always include the district in the citation, never the division.

In general, for state decisions the state and the name of the court should be included within the parentheses. However, do not include the name of the court if the court of decision is the highest court of the state. Here is an example of how to cite a Pennsylvania Supreme Court case. How do you know what to include in the parentheses? Read Rule 10.4(b) and look at the listing for Pennsylvania in table T.1. **Example: *Commonwealth v. Brayboy*, 246 A.2d 675 (Pa. 1968).**

Find 98 P.3d 381 to answer Questions 6 and 7.

6.   State the full citation for 98 P.3d 381.

Should you ever cite the official version of a case? Yes, if the case is very old and there is no regional citation. Otherwise, you should cite it **only** if you are **including it in a document submitted to a state court whose local rules require citation to the official reporter.** (See Rule 10.3.1(a), Bluepages B5.1.3, and table BT.2.) Here is our previous example cited in such a context. **Example:** *Commonwealth v. Brayboy,* **431 Pa. 365, 246 A.2d 675 (1968).** Note: We followed Rule 10.4(b) and omitted the jurisdiction Pa. from the parentheses because it is unambiguously conveyed by the reporter title.

7.   State the full citation for 98 P.3d 381, assuming you are including this citation in a document submitted to an Oregon state court whose local rules require citing to the official report volume.

Next, find an opinion from a state intermediate appellate court and cite it correctly. **Example:** *Maluszewski v. Allstate Ins. Co.,* **640 A.2d 129 (Conn. App. Ct. 1994).**

Find 816 N.E.2d 1010 to answer Questions 8 and 9.

8.   State the full citation for 816 N.E.2d 1010.

Our previous example of an intermediate state appellate court citation cited in a document submitted to a Connecticut state court whose local rules require citing to the official report volume would look like this. **Example:** *Maluszewski v. Allstate Ins. Co.,* **34 Conn. App. 27, 640 A.2d 129 (1994).**

9.   State the full citation for 816 N.E.2d 1010, assuming you are including this citation in a document to a Massachusetts state court whose local rules require citing to the official report volume.

ASSIGNMENT ONE
FINDING AND CITING CASES
EXERCISE D

GOALS OF THIS ASSIGNMENT:
To teach you how to find cases when you have citations.
To acquaint you with the location of reporters in your law library.
To familiarize you with the rules for citing cases in *The Bluebook: A Uniform System of Citation*, 18th ed.

CITATION RULES: Read the *Introduction*, Bluepages B1, Bluepages B5.1- B5.1.3, Rules 6.1, 10.2.1, 10.2.2, 10.3.1, 10.3.2, 10.4, 10.5 and refer to tables BT.2, T.1, T.6, and T.10 of *The Bluebook*. Apply these rules as you learn the correct citation for each case.
Throughout this book, when we ask that you provide a full citation, give the name, citation and date of the case, and any other necessary information (such as court) required by *The Bluebook*.

The first two questions introduce you to the rules for citing U.S. Supreme Court cases. **Example: *Loving v. Virginia*, 388 U.S. 1 (1967).**

United States Reports, abbreviated U.S. in case citation, is the official reporter. Note that no parallel, unofficial reporters are listed for U.S. Supreme Court cases when a U.S. citation is available. At the beginning of table T.1 in *The Bluebook*, read the instructions for the **Supreme Court**.

1.   If an opinion of the U.S. Supreme Court has not yet been published in *United States Reports*, which unofficial reporters should you cite instead, in order of preference?

2.   State the full citation for 536 U.S. 730.

The third question requires you to find and cite a U.S. Supreme Court case from before 1875. They published these cases in reporters known as **nominative** reporters, because they were generally known by the name of the person who compiled the volume. The form of citation for a case in a nominative reporter differs from the form for a case appearing in contemporary sources. Study the rules for citing cases found in nominative reporters (*The Bluebook* calls them "early American reporters." See Rule 10.3.2.). Here is an example of how to cite a U.S. Supreme Court nominative reporter: ***Hughes v. Union Ins. Co.*, 21 U.S. (8 Wheat.) 294 (1823).**

3.   State the full citation for 49 U.S. 124. Note: For the date, use the year of the Court Term.

Next, you must find and cite a federal court of appeals case from a circuit. When citing a court of appeals case always list the circuit within the parentheses, along with the date. **Example: Bonilla v. Volvo Car Corp., 150 F.3d 62 (1st Cir. 1998).**

4.   State the full citation for 361 F.3d 449.

Now, find and cite a federal district court case. When citing a case from district court, the particular court is included within the parentheses. **Example: Hillard v. Guidant Corp., 76 F. Supp. 2d 566 (M.D. Pa. 1999).**

5.   State the full citation for 301 F. Supp. 2d 454. Note: The district is listed before the state—the division, if listed, is listed after. Always include the district in the citation, never the division.

In general, for state decisions the state and the name of the court should be included within the parentheses. However, do not include the name of the court if the court of decision is the highest court of the state. Here is an example of how to cite a Pennsylvania Supreme Court case. How do you know what to include in the parentheses? Read Rule 10.4(b) and look at the listing for Pennsylvania in table T.1. **Example: Commonwealth v. Brayboy, 246 A.2d 675 (Pa. 1968).**

Find 84 P.3d 509 to answer Questions 6 and 7.

6.   State the full citation for 84 P.3d 509.

Should you ever cite the official version of a case? Yes, if the case is very old and there is no regional citation. Otherwise, you should cite it **only** if you are **including it in a document submitted to a state court whose local rules require citation to the official reporter.** (See Rule 10.3.1(a), Bluepages B5.1.3, and table BT.2.) Here is our previous example cited in such a context. **Example:** ***Commonwealth v. Brayboy,* 431 Pa. 365, 246 A.2d 675 (1968).** Note: We followed Rule 10.4(b) and omitted the jurisdiction Pa. from the parentheses because it is unambiguously conveyed by the reporter title.

7.   State the full citation for 84 P.3d 509, assuming you are including this citation in a document submitted to a Hawaii state court whose local rules require citing to the official report volume.

Next, find an opinion from a state intermediate appellate court and cite it correctly. **Example: *Maluszewski v. Allstate Ins. Co.*, 640 A.2d 129 (Conn. App. Ct. 1994).**

Find 725 A.2d 623 to answer Questions 8 and 9.

8.   State the full citation for 725 A.2d 623.

Our previous example of an intermediate state appellate court citation cited in a document submitted to a Connecticut state court whose local rules require citing to the official report volume would look like this. **Example: *Maluszewski v. Allstate Ins. Co.*, 34 Conn. App. 27, 640 A.2d 129 (1994).**

9.   State the full citation for 725 A.2d 623, assuming you are including this citation in a document to a Maryland state court whose local rules require citing to the official report volume.

ASSIGNMENT TWO
SUPREME COURT REPORTERS AND PARTS OF A CASE
EXERCISE A

GOALS OF THIS ASSIGNMENT:
To familiarize you with the parts of a case in three different reporters.
To introduce you to star paging.

CITATION RULES: Use *The Bluebook: A Uniform System of Citation*, 18th ed., Rules 10.2, 10.2.1, 10.2.2, 10.3.1, 10.3.2, 10.4, 10.5 and tables T.1, T.6 and T.10. Use the format for court documents and legal memoranda and assume that the case citation appears in a citation sentence.

Locate 493 U.S. 521 to answer Questions 1-9.

1.   Find 493 U.S. 521. This is the official reporter version of the case. What is the case name? Use correct form (Rule 10.2).

2.   On what date was the case decided?

3.   What is the docket number of the case?

4.   Which party is the respondent?

5.   Which Justice wrote the majority opinion?

6.   Which Justice wrote the dissenting opinion?

7.   What was the lower court cite of this case, on its way up to the Supreme Court? Note: You are looking for the cite of a F.2d case.

8.   How did the Supreme Court act on the judgment of the court below?

9.   Who argued the cause for the petitioner?

To answer Questions 10-17 you will need to compare the case from Question 1 in the two unofficial versions, S. Ct., L. Ed., of this opinion.

10.   Find the appropriate book of vol. 110 of the *Supreme Court Reporter* (S. Ct.), published by West, and vol. 107 of the *U.S. Supreme Court Reports--Lawyers' Edition* (L. Ed. 2d), published by LexisNexis. These two reporters are unofficial reporters for United States Supreme Court cases. Use the Cases Reported table at the front of S. Ct. and the Table of Cases Reported in the front of L. Ed. to find your case in both reporters.

      a.   What is the S. Ct. cite?

      b.   What is the L. Ed. cite?

11.   Examine the headnotes preceding the opinions. On which page of which reporter does the seventh West topic and key number appear? (Note: A small key-shaped symbol accompanies the West topic and key number.)

12. State the West topic and key number from the preceding question.

13. Each headnote corresponds to a particular part of the Court's opinion. Examine the opinion in S. Ct. and look for references to the headnote numbers (boldface numbers in brackets **[1]**). On which page of the S. Ct. **opinion** is there a reference to the seventh West headnote?

14. Star paging enables attorneys using L. Ed. or S. Ct. to cite U.S. paging without having U.S. itself. Star paging in L. Ed. is shown thus: **[405 US 729]**. Star paging in S. Ct. is indicated thus: ⊥**729**. Looking at the *Supreme Court Reporter* and using star paging ⊥, state on which page of *United States Reports* (U.S.) you will find the corresponding material related to the seventh **[7]** West headnote.

15. Notice that the two unofficial reporters have different headnotes. How many headnotes are in the *U.S. Supreme Court Reports, Lawyers' Edition*?

16. Question 8 asked you about the **disposition** of the case, that is, how the Supreme Court treated the judgment of the court below. The **holding** is another part of a case, the application of rules of law to the specific key facts in the case. Did the court hold that the child-disability regulations were inconsistent with the statutory standard of "comparable severity"? You may want to review the syllabus of the case.

17. What law authorizes Supplemental Security Income benefits to a child who suffers from an impairment of "comparable severity" to one that would render an adult disabled?

ASSIGNMENT TWO
SUPREME COURT REPORTERS AND PARTS OF A CASE
EXERCISE B

GOALS OF THIS ASSIGNMENT:
To familiarize you with the parts of a case in three different reporters.
To introduce you to star paging.

CITATION RULES: Use *The Bluebook: A Uniform System of Citation*, 18th ed., Rules 10.2, 10.2.1, 10.2.2, 10.3.1, 10.3.2, 10.4, 10.5 and tables T.1, T.6 and T.10. Use the format for court documents and legal memoranda and assume that the case citation appears in a citation sentence.

Locate 526 U.S. 813 to answer Questions 1-9.

1.   Find 526 U.S. 813. This is the official reporter version of the case. What is the case name? Use correct form (Rule 10.2).

2.   On what date was the case decided?

3.   What is the docket number of the case?

4.   Which party is the petitioner?

5.   Which Justice wrote the opinion of the court?

6.   Which Justice wrote a dissenting opinion?

7. What was the lower court cite of this case, on its way up to the Supreme Court? Note: You are looking for the cite of a F.3d case.

8. How did the Supreme Court act on the judgment of the court below?

9. Who argued the cause for the petitioner?

To answer Questions 10-17, you will need to compare the case from Question 1 in the two unofficial versions, S. Ct., L. Ed., of this opinion.

10. Find the appropriate book of vol. 119 of the *Supreme Court Reporter* (S. Ct.), published by West, and vol. 143 of the *U.S. Supreme Court Reports—Lawyers' Edition* (L. Ed. 2d), published then by Lexis Publishing and now by LexisNexis. These two reporters are unofficial reporters for United States Supreme Court cases. Use the Cases Reported table at the front of S. Ct. and the Table of Cases Reported in the front of L. Ed. to find your case in both reporters.

    a. What is the S. Ct. cite?

    b. What is the L. Ed. cite?

11. Examine the headnotes preceding the opinions. On what page of which reporter does the third West topic and key number appear? (Note: A small key-shaped symbol accompanies the West topic and key number.)

12.   State the West topic and key number from the preceding question.

13.   Each headnote corresponds to a particular part of the Court's opinion. Examine the opinion in S. Ct. and look for references to the headnote numbers (boldface numbers in brackets [1]). On what page of the S. Ct. **opinion** is there a reference to the third West headnote?

14.   Star paging enables attorneys using L. Ed. or S. Ct. to cite U.S. paging without using U.S. itself. Star paging in L. Ed. is shown thus: **[405 US 729]**. Star paging in S. Ct. is indicated thus: ⊥**729.** Looking at the *Supreme Court Reporter* and using star paging ⊥, state the page of *United States Reports* (U.S.) on which the corresponding material related to the third **[3]** West headnote begins.

15.   Notice that the two unofficial reporters have different headnotes. How many headnotes are in the *U.S. Supreme Court Reports, Lawyers' Edition*?

16.   Question 8 asked you about the **disposition** of the case, that is, how the Supreme Court treated the judgment of the court below. The **holding** is another part of a case, the application of rules of law to the specific key facts in the case. Did the court hold that a jury in a § 848 case must unanimously agree not only that the defendant committed some "continuing series of violations," but also about which specific "violations" make up that "continuing series"? You may want to review the syllabus of the case.

17.   In what title of the United States Code (U.S.C.) is § 848, the section at issue in this case located? [Hint: The U.S. Code is arranged in fifty subjects, each known as a numerical Title. You are looking for the numerical title in which section 848 is located.]

ASSIGNMENT TWO
SUPREME COURT REPORTERS AND PARTS OF A CASE
EXERCISE C

GOALS OF THIS ASSIGNMENT:
To familiarize you with the parts of a case in three different reporters.
To introduce you to star paging.

CITATION RULES: Use *The Bluebook: A Uniform System of Citation*, 18th ed., Rules 10.2, 10.2.1, 10.2.2, 10.3.1, 10.3.2, 10.4, 10.5 and tables T.1, T.6 and T.10. Use the format for court documents and legal memoranda and assume that the case citation appears in a citation sentence.

Locate 537 U.S. 322 to answer Questions 1-9.

1. Find 537 U.S. 322. This is the official reporter version of the case. What is the case name? Use correct form (Rule 10.2).

2. On what date was the case decided?

3. What is the docket number of the case?

4. Which party is the respondent?

5. Which Justice wrote the opinion of the court?

6. Which Justice wrote a dissenting opinion?

7.   What was the lower court cite of this case, on its way up to the Supreme Court? Note: You are looking for the cite of a F.3d case.

8.   How did the Supreme Court act on the judgment of the court below?

9.   Who argued the cause for the petitioner?

To answer Questions 10-17 you will need to compare the case from Question 1 in the two unofficial versions, S. Ct., L. Ed., of this opinion.

10.   Find the appropriate book of vol. 123 of the *Supreme Court Reporter* (S. Ct.), published by West, and vol. 154 of the *U.S. Supreme Court Reports—Lawyers' Edition* (L. Ed. 2d), published then by Lexis Publishing and now by LexisNexis. These two reporters are unofficial reporters for United States Supreme Court cases. Use the Cases Reported table at the front of S. Ct. and the Table of Cases Reported in the front of L. Ed. to find your case in both reporters.

        a. What is the S. Ct. cite?

        b. What is the L. Ed. cite?

11.   Examine the headnotes preceding the opinions. On what page of which reporter does the ninth West topic and key number appear? (Note: A small key-shaped symbol accompanies the West topic and key number.)

12.   State the West topic and key number from the preceding question.

13.   Each headnote corresponds to a particular part of the Court's opinion. Examine the opinion in S. Ct. and look for references to the headnote numbers (boldface numbers in brackets [1]). On what page of the S. Ct. **opinion** is there a reference to the ninth West headnote?

14.   Star paging enables attorneys using L. Ed. or S. Ct. to cite U.S. paging without using U.S. itself. Star paging in L. Ed. is shown thus: **[405 US 729]**. Star paging in S. Ct. is indicated thus: $\perp$**729** Looking at the *Supreme Court Reporter* and using star paging $\perp$, state the page of *United States Reports* (U.S.) on which the corresponding material related to the ninth **[9]** West headnote begins.

15.   Notice that the two unofficial reporters have different headnotes. How many headnotes are in the *U.S. Supreme Court Reports, Lawyers' Edition*?

16.   Question 8 asked you about the **disposition** of the case, that is, how the Supreme Court treated the judgment of the court below. The **holding** is another part of a case, the application of rules of law to the specific key facts in the case. Did the court hold that the Fifth Circuit should have issued a certificate of appealability to review the District Court's denial of habeas relief to petritioner? You may want to review the syllabus of the case.

17.   Under which section of Title 28 of U.S.C. did the petitioner in this case apply for a certificate of appealability? [Hint: Titles of the U.S. Code are divided into chapters and then into sections which are identified numerically. You are looking for a numerical section of Title 28.]

ASSIGNMENT TWO
SUPREME COURT REPORTERS AND PARTS OF A CASE
EXERCISE D

GOALS OF THIS ASSIGNMENT:
To familiarize you with the parts of a case in three different reporters.
To introduce you to star paging.

CITATION RULES: Use *The Bluebook: A Uniform System of Citation*, 18th ed., Rules 10.2, 10.2.1, 10.2.2, 10.3.1, 10.3.2, 10.4, 10.5 and tables T.1, T.6 and T.10. Use the format for court documents and legal memoranda and assume that the case citation appears in a citation sentence.

Locate 503 U.S. 1 to answer Questions 1-9.

1.   Find 503 U.S. 1. This is the official reporter version of the case. What is the case name? Use correct form (Rule 10.2).

2.   On what date was the case decided?

3.   What is the docket number of the case?

4.   Which party is the petitioner?

5.   Which Justice wrote the opinion of the court?

6.   Which Justice wrote a dissenting opinion?

7.   What was the lower court cite of this case, on its way up to the Supreme Court? Note: You are looking for the cite of a F.2d case.

8.   How did the Supreme Court act on the judgment of the court below?

9.   Who argued the cause for the petitioner?

      To answer Questions 10-17, you will need to compare the case from Question 1 in the two unofficial versions, S. Ct., L. Ed., of this opinion.

10.   Find the appropriate book of vol. 112 of the *Supreme Court Reporter* (S. Ct.), published by West, and vol. 117 of the *U.S. Supreme Court Reports—Lawyers' Edition* (L. Ed. 2d), published then by Lexis Law Publishing and now by LexisNexis. These two reporters are unofficial reporters for United States Supreme Court cases. Use the Cases Reported table at the front of S. Ct. and the Table of Cases Reported in the front of L. Ed. to find your case in both reporters.

      a. What is the S. Ct. cite?

      b. What is the L. Ed. cite?

11.   Examine the headnotes preceding the opinions. On what page of which reporter does the fifth West topic and key number appear? (Note: A small key-shaped symbol accompanies the West topic and key number.)

12.   State the West topic and key number from the preceding question.

13.   Each headnote corresponds to a particular part of the Court's opinion. Examine the opinion in S. Ct. and look for references to the headnote numbers (boldface numbers in brackets [1]). On what page of the S. Ct. **opinion** is there a reference to the fifth West headnote?

14.   Star paging enables attorneys using L. Ed. or S. Ct. to cite U.S. paging without using U.S. itself. Star paging in L. Ed. is shown thus: **[405 US 729]**. Star paging in S. Ct. is indicated thus: ⊥**729**   Looking at the *Supreme Court Reporter* and using star paging ⊥, state the page of *United States Reports* (U.S.) on which the corresponding material related to the fifth **[5]** West headnote begins.

15.   Notice that the two unofficial reporters have different headnotes. How many headnotes are in the *U.S. Supreme Court Reports, Lawyers' Edition*?

16.   Question 8 asked you about the **disposition** of the case, that is, how the Supreme Court treated the judgment of the court below. The **holding** is another part of a case, the application of rules of law to the specific key facts in the case. Did the court hold that use of excessive force may constitute cruel and unusual punishment even though the inmate does not suffer serious injury? You may want to review the syllabus of the case.

17.   Which U.S. Constitutional provision prohibits cruel and unusual punishment?

ASSIGNMENT THREE
REGIONAL REPORTERS
EXERCISE A

GOALS OF THIS ASSIGNMENT:
To acquaint you with the Table of Cases in the digests.
To compare the features of regional reporters.

CITATION RULES: For this assignment when citing a case, assume you are citing the case in a legal document that will be submitted to a state court that does not require parallel cites.

Assume you want to find the unofficial (regional) text of *Anderson v. Heartland Oil & Gas, Inc.*, a 1991 Supreme Court of Kansas case. When you know the case name and jurisdiction, but do not know the citation, one way to find the citation is to look it up in a digest table of cases. Look up *Anderson v. Heartland Oil & Gas, Inc.* in the Table of Cases volume in either the *Kansas Digest 2d*, the *Pacific Digest* (Beginning 585 P.2d) or the *Tenth Decennial Digest, Part 2*.

1. What is the full citation of the case? (Remember, this means name, cite, jurisdiction, court and year according to Rule 10 of *The Bluebook*.)

Find the unofficial report of the case in the *Pacific Reporter* and answer Questions 2-8.

2. Notice the long, one-paragraph summary of the facts and holding. This is called the synopsis and West editors wrote it. According to the synopsis, how did the Supreme Court dispose of the decision of the District Court?

3. Notice the headnotes (one-sentence summaries of points of law). All headnotes in the regional reporters that follow West topic and key numbers are written by West editors. How many headnotes are listed here?

4. A topic and key number precede each headnote in a regional reporter, like those you saw in Assignment Two. What is the topic and key number for the ninth headnote?

Never quote from or cite to the synopsis or headnotes. You can, however, search them on WESTLAW, along with the topics and key numbers. Cases are divided into different parts, called **fields** on WESTLAW and **segments** on LEXIS. Fields and segments can be searched separately, or with the rest of the case.

5. Remember, you can find the part of the opinion that corresponds to the ninth headnote by looking for the corresponding boldface number in brackets in the opinion. On what page of the opinion do you find the corresponding text for the ninth headnote?

6. Read the opinion. Did the court hold that doing business in the state supplies minimum contact required for a nonresident to be subject to personal jurisdiction under the Kansas long arm statute?

7. Look at the beginning of the case. What is the official cite, which is given just above the name of the case?

8. Look at the title page of the *Pacific Reporter* volume. List **five** states covered in the *Pacific Reporter*.

9. Using your textbook or *The Bluebook: A Uniform System of Citation*, state the regional reporters in which the following states' cases are found:

    a. Alaska

    b. Louisiana

    c. Texas

In this assignment, you used the table of cases in a digest to find the cite to a case. You then found that case in a regional reporter. Does your own state have an official reporter? Check table T.1 in *The Bluebook* or ask your instructor.

ASSIGNMENT THREE
REGIONAL REPORTERS
EXERCISE B

GOALS OF THIS ASSIGNMENT:
To acquaint you with the Table of Cases in the digests.
To compare the features of regional reporters.

CITATION RULES: For this assignment when citing a case, assume you are citing the case in a legal document that will be submitted to a state court that does not require parallel cites.

Assume you want to find the unofficial (regional) text of *Bromund v. Holt*, a 1964 Wisconsin Supreme Court case. When you know the case name and jurisdiction, but do not know the citation, one way to find the citation is to look it up in a digest table of cases. Look up *Bromund v. Hold* in the Table of Cases volume in either the *Wisconsin Digest*, the *North Western Digest 2d* or the *Seventh Decennial Digest*.

1.   What is the full citation of the case? (Remember, this means name, cite, jurisdiction, court and year according to Rule 10 of *The Bluebook*.)

        Find the unofficial report of the case in the *North Western Reporter* and answer Questions 2-8.

2.   Notice the long, one-paragraph summary of the facts and holding. This is called the synopsis and West editors wrote it. According to the synopsis, how did the Supreme Court dispose of the decision of the Circuit Court?

3.   Notice the headnotes (one-sentence summaries of points of law). All headnotes in the regional reporters that follow West topic and key numbers are written by West editors. How many headnotes are listed here?

4.   A topic and key number precede each headnote in a regional reporter, like those you saw in Assignment Two. What is the topic and key number for the ninth headnote?

35

Never quote from or cite to the synopsis or headnotes. You can, however, search them on WESTLAW, along with the topics and key numbers. Cases are divided into different parts, called **fields** on WESTLAW and **segments** on LEXIS. Fields and segments can be searched separately, or with the rest of the case.

5.   Remember, you can find the part of the opinion that corresponds to the ninth headnote by looking for the corresponding boldface number in brackets in the opinion. On what page of the opinion do you find the corresponding text for the ninth headnote?

6.   Read the opinion. What did the court state are the two elements essential to a cause of action for malicious prosecution?

7.   Look at the beginning of the case. What is the official cite, which is given just above the name of the case?

8.   Look at the title page of a *North Western Reporter* volume. List the **seven** states covered in the *North Western Reporter*.

9.   Using your textbook or *The Bluebook: A Uniform System of Citation*, state the regional reporters in which the following states' cases are found:

        a. Arizona

        b. Indiana

        c. Virginia

In this assignment, you used the table of cases in a digest to find the cite to a case. You then found that case in a regional reporter. Does your own state have an official reporter? Check table T.1 in *The Bluebook* or ask your instructor.

GOALS OF THIS ASSIGNMENT:
To acquaint you with the Table of Cases in the digests.
To compare the features of regional reporters.

CITATION RULES: For this assignment when citing a case, assume you are citing the case in a legal document that will be submitted to a state court that does not require parallel cites.

Assume you want to find the unofficial (regional) text of *O'Brien v. DeKalb County*, a 1987 Supreme Court of Georgia case. When you know the case name and jurisdiction, but do not know the citation, one way to find the citation is to look it up in a digest table of cases. Look up *O'Brien v. DeKalb County* in the Table of Cases volume in either the *Georgia Digest 2d,* the *South Eastern Digest 2d* or the *Tenth Decennial Digest, Part 1*.

1.   What is the full citation of the case? (Remember, this means name, cite, jurisdiction, court and year according to Rule 10 of *The Bluebook*.)

Find the unofficial report of the case in the *South Eastern Reporter* and answer Questions 2-8.

2.   Notice the long, one-paragraph summary of the facts and holding. This is called the synopsis and West editors wrote it. According to the synopsis, how did the Supreme Court dispose of the decision of the DeKalb Recorders Court?

3.   Notice the headnotes (one-sentence summaries of points of law). All headnotes in the regional reporters that follow West topic and key numbers are written by West editors. How many headnotes are listed here?

4.   A topic and key number precede each headnote in a regional reporter, like those you saw in Assignment Two. What is the topic and key number for the second headnote?

Never quote from or cite to the synopsis or headnotes. You can, however, search them on WESTLAW, along with the topics and key numbers. Cases are divided into different parts, called **fields** on WESTLAW and **segments** on LEXIS. Fields and segments can be searched separately, or with the rest of the case.

5.   Remember, you can find the part of the opinion that corresponds to the second headnote by looking for the corresponding boldface number in brackets in the opinion. On what page of the opinion do you find the corresponding text for the second headnote?

6.   Read the opinion. What two DeKalb County Code ordinances were involved in this case?

7.   Look at the beginning of the case. What is the official cite, which is given just above the name of the case?

8.   Look at the title page of the *South Eastern Reporter* volume. List the **five** states covered in the *South Eastern Reporter*.

9.   Using you textbook or *The Bluebook: A Uniform System of Citation*, state the regional reporters in which the following states' cases are found:

        a. Delaware

        b. Massachusetts

        c. Tennessee

In this assignment, you used the table of cases in a digest to find the cite to a case. You then found that case in a regional reporter. Does your own state have an official reporter? Check table T.1 in *The Bluebook* or ask your instructor.

ASSIGNMENT THREE
REGIONAL REPORTERS
EXERCISE D

GOALS OF THIS ASSIGNMENT:
To acquaint you with the Table of Cases in the digests.
To compare the features of regional reporters.

CITATION RULES: For this assignment when citing a case, assume you are citing the case in a legal document that will be submitted to a state court that does not require parallel cites.

Assume you want to find the unofficial (regional) text of *Macysyn v. Hensler, Inc.*, a 2000 Superior Court of New Jersey, Appellate Division case. When you know the case name and jurisdiction, but do not know the citation, one way to find the citation is to look it up in a digest table of cases. Look up *Macysyn v. Hensler* in the Table of Cases volume in either the *New Jersey Digest 2d*, the *Atlantic Digest 2d*, or the *Eleventh Decennial Digest, Part 1*.

1.   What is the full citation of the case? (Remember, this means name, cite, jurisdiction, court and year according to Rule 10 of *The Bluebook*.)

    Find the unofficial report of the case in the *Atlantic Reporter* and answer Questions 2-8.

2.   Notice the long, one-paragraph summary of the facts and holding. This is called the synopsis and West editors wrote it. According to the synopsis, how did the Supreme Court dispose of the Division of Workers' Compensation decision?

3.   Notice the headnotes (one-sentence summaries of points of law). All headnotes in the regional reporters that follow West topic and key numbers are written by West editors. How many headnotes are listed here?

4.   A topic and key number precede each headnote in a regional reporter, like those you saw in Assignment Two. What is the topic and key number for the second headnote?

Never quote from or cite to the synopsis or headnotes. You can, however, search them on WESTLAW, along with the topics and key numbers. Cases are divided into different parts, called **fields** on WESTLAW and **segments** on LEXIS. Fields and segments can be searched separately, or with the rest of the case.

5.   Remember, you can find the part of the opinion that corresponds to the second headnote by looking for the corresponding boldface number in brackets in the opinion. On what page of the opinion do you find the corresponding text for the second headnote?

6.   Read the opinion. As to the Division of Workers' Compensation's subject matter jurisdiction, the court quoted which statute as giving the Division "the exclusive original jurisdiction of all claims for workers' compensation benefits under this chapter"?

7.   Look at the beginning of the case. What is the official cite, which is given just above the name of the case?

8.   Look at the title page of the *Atlantic Reporter* volume. List **five** states covered in the *Atlantic Reporter*.

9.   Using your textbook or *The Bluebook: A Uniform System of Citation*, state the regional reporters in which the following states' cases are found:

            a. Arkansas

            b. Florida

            c. Minnesota

In this assignment, you used the table of cases in a digest to find the cite to a case. You then found that case in a regional reporter. Does your own state have an official reporter? Check table T.1 in *The Bluebook* or ask your instructor.

ASSIGNMENT FOUR
FINDING CASES–DIGESTS
EXERCISE A

GOALS OF THIS ASSIGNMENT:
To introduce you to West digests.
To give you practice at the various methods of using digests.

CITATION RULES: For this assignment when citing a case, assume you are citing the case in a legal document that will be submitted to a state court that does not require parallel cites.

Please research Kansas corporate law cases. We need to know under what circumstances courts have held that minority stockholders having standing to sue majority stockholders of the same corporation for damages. Another attorney has given you a relevant case, *Richards v. Bryan*, a 1994 Court of Appeals of Kansas case which has a headnote on point. Use this case to find other relevant cases. This is called the "one good case" approach. Check the Table of Cases in either 1) the *Kansas Digest 2d*; 2) the *Pacific Digest* (Beginning 585 P.2d); or 3) the *Tenth Decennial Digest, Part 2* (in that order of preference) to find the regional cite for the case.

1.   What is the regional cite for the case?

2.   Look up the case in the regional reporter. The relevant headnote for our issue is headnote sixteen. What is the West topic and key number of headnote sixteen?

3.   We now have a West topic and key number to begin our digest research. First, let's find out just what this topic and key number represent. Find the analysis outline at the very beginning of the topic from Question 2 in your digest. Examine the list of key numbers. What does the key number from Question 2 stand for? Include all relevant topics of which your key number may be a subtopic.

41

You will be using the same digest to answer Questions 4-11a or 4-11b.

4. Go to your key number and look at the cases listed under it. Is there a Supreme Court of Kansas case from 1995 digested under this topic and key number? If so, provide the full regional citation of the case according to Rule 10 of *The Bluebook*.

5. Now you will use the topic approach. The topic approach merely involves reading the list of key numbers at the beginning of the topic (the topic outline) and looking for relevant key numbers. Go back to the topic outline (called "Analysis") for **Corporations**. If you were looking for cases concerning the general nature and grounds for which members and stockholders are liable for corporate debts and acts, under what topic and key number would you look?

6. Look up that key number. State the name of the 1992 Supreme Court of Kansas case as listed.

7. Now you will use the subject approach. Look in the Descriptive Word Index volumes (either at the beginning or the end of the set). Using the descriptive word approach, find the topic and key number for cases dealing with the status of a corporation as a citizen. To what topic and key number are you referred?

8. Look up the topic and key number and find a 1995 Supreme Court of Kansas case. List the full regional citation of the case in correct form.

SECTION I: Complete Questions 9a-13a in Section I if you used a state or regional digest for this assignment.

HOW TO UPDATE YOUR DIGEST RESEARCH IF YOU ARE USING A STATE OR REGIONAL DIGEST

Step 1. Current digest volumes are supplemented by annual pocket parts. Look in the pocket part for your topic and key number.

OR

If the pocket part is too thick to fit in the volume, the pocket part becomes a free standing pamphlet that updates that particular volume. Look in the pamphlet for your topic and key number.

Step 2. Depending on how recently the annual pocket parts were issued, your digest may have a pamphlet that directly supplements the annual pocket parts. If so, look up your topic and key number in this pamphlet.

Step 3. If the digest has a supplemental pamphlet from Step 2, check the "Closing with Cases Reported in" section on the second page of the pamphlet. If there is not a supplemental pamphlet, check the "Closing with Cases Reported in" section on the second page of the pocket part/pamphlet from Step 1.

Step 4. Go the reporter volume that you identified in Step 3. Beginning with the volume listed in the "Closing with Cases Reported in" from Step 3, look in the digest sections in the back of all bound volumes and in the front of all advance sheets to see if any recent cases have appeared under your topic and key number.

9a.   Does your digest volume have a pocket part or pamphlet as explained in Step 1? If so, look up the topic and key number from Question 7. Are there any cases from Kansas digested under this topic and key number?

10a.   Does your digest have a supplemental pamphlet as explained in Step 2? If so, look up the topic and key number from Question 7. Are there any cases from Kansas digested under this topic and key number?

11a.   Perform Step 3 of updating the digest by looking at the "Closing with Cases Reported in" statement on the second page of the supplemental pamphlet for the digest if there are any. If not, look at the "Closing with Cases Reported in" on the second page of the pocket part/pamphlet. According to the "Closing with Cases Reported in," what is the last volume of P.3d that the digest pocket part/pamphlet covers?

Now go to the *Pacific Reporter 3d* and find the volume from Question 11a.

12a.   Each bound reporter volume has a small digest section in the back which gives you the topics and key numbers for the cases printed in that volume. Normally, you would check the digest sections of all of the bound reporters beginning with the volume from Question 11a. For this assignment, however, check **only** the **most recent** bound volume. Are there any Kansas cases digested under your topic and key number?

13a.   Now check the *Pacific Reporter's* advance sheets. Bound volumes are updated by paperbound advance sheets. Several advance sheets are bound together into a reporter. In advance sheets, the digest section is in the front, just before the decisions begin. Normally, you would look at the digest section in all of the advance sheets for your topic and key number. For this assignment, however, check **only** the **most recent** advance sheet. Are there any Kansas cases are digested under your topic and key number?

SECTION II: Complete Questions 9b-13b in Section II if you used a Decennial Digest for this assignment.

HOW TO UPDATE YOUR DIGEST RESEARCH IF YOU ARE USING A DECENNIAL DIGEST:

Step 1. Look for your topic and key number in all of the subsequent Decennial Digests that were issued after the one you used in this assignment.

Step 2. The most recent Decennial Digest is updated by the General Digest. You will need to look at every volume of the General Digest for your topic and key number.

Step 3. Check the "Closing with Cases Reported in" on the second page of the last General Digest on the shelf.

Step 4. Go the reporter volume that you identified in Step 3. Beginning with the volume listed in the "Closing with Cases Reported in" from Step 3, look in the digest sections in the back of all bound volumes and in the front of all advance sheets to see if any recent cases have appeared under your topic and key number.

9b. Are there any subsequent Decennial Digests since the Decennial Digest you used in this exercise? If so, look up the topic and key number from Question 7 in each subsequent Decennial Digest. Are there any cases from Kansas digested under this topic and key number?

10b. Find the General Digests. Look up the topic and key number from Question 7 in each volume of the General Digest. Are there any cases from Kansas digested under this topic and key number?

11b. Perform Step 3 of updating the digest by looking at the "Closing with Cases Reported in" statement on the second page of the last General Digest on the shelf. According to the "Closing with Cases Reported in," what is the last volume of P.3d that this volume of the General Digest covers?

Now go to the *Pacific Reporter 3d* and find the volume from Question 11b.

12b. Each bound reporter volume has a small digest section in the back which gives you the topics and key numbers for the cases printed in that volume. Normally, you would check the digest sections of all of the bound reporters beginning with the volume from Question 11b. For this assignment, however, check **only** the **most recent** bound volume. Are there any Kansas cases digested under your topic and key number?

13b.   Now check the *Pacific Reporter's* advance sheets. Bound volumes are updated by paperbound advance sheets. Several advance sheets are bound together into a reporter. In advance sheets, the digest section is in the front, just before the decisions begin. Normally, you would look at the digest section in all of the advance sheets for your topic and key number. For this assignment, however, check **only** the **most recent** advance sheet. Are there any Kansas cases digested under your topic and key number?

One great advantage of the West topic and key number system is that you can use it for **all jurisdictions**. The same topic and key number can be used for researching all state and federal courts whose decisions are published in West reporters. Different West digests will group jurisdictions in different ways. For example, the *Kansas Digest* contains Kansas cases and federal cases arising in Kansas. Each West state digest has similar coverage.

Regional digests contain state cases from each state covered by that particular region. The federal digests cover all of the federal courts, and the Decennial and General Digests, all of the state and federal jurisdictions. Use the most appropriate digest in your library, and provide the full citation, in correct form, for the following cases. Search under the topic and key number from **Question 2**.

14.   Check the *Maine Digest*, the *Atlantic Digest 2d*, or the *Tenth Decennial Digest, Part 2*. Provide the full regional citation, in correct form, of the 1994 Maine Supreme Court case digested under the topic and key number from Question 2.

15.   Check the *Federal Practice Digest 4th*. Is there a 1996 Eighth Circuit Court of Appeals cases arising from Missouri digested under this topic and key number? If so, provide the full citation in correct form.

ASSIGNMENT FOUR
FINDING CASES–DIGESTS
EXERCISE B

GOALS OF THIS ASSIGNMENT:
To introduce you to West digests.
To give you practice at the various methods of using digests.

CITATION RULES: For this assignment when citing a case, assume you are citing the case in a legal document that will be submitted to a state court that does not require parallel cites.

Please research Wisconsin cases to find cases discussing that the essential elements in an action for malicious prosecution must include the lack of probable cause in instituting the proceeding. Another attorney has given you a relevant case, *Pollock v. Vilter Mfg. Corp.,* a 1964 Supreme Court of Wisconsin case which has a headnote on point. Use this case to find other relevant cases. This is called the "one good case" approach. Check the Table of Cases in either 1) the *Wisconsin Digest*; 2) the *North Western Digest 2d*; or 3) the *Seventh Decennial Digest* (in that order of preference) to find the regional cite for the case.

1.   What is the regional cite for the case?

2.   Look up the case in the regional reporter. The relevant headnote for our issue is headnote two. What is the West topic and key number of headnote two?

3.   We now have a West topic and key number to begin our digest research. First, let's find out just what this topic and key number represent. Find the analysis outline at the very beginning of the topic from Question 2 in your digest. Examine the list of key numbers. What does the key number from Question 2 stand for? Include all relevant topics of which your key number may be a subtopic.

You will be using the same digest to answer Questions 4-11a or 4-11b.

4.   Go to your key number and look at the cases listed under it. Is there a Wisconsin Supreme Court case from 1960 digested under this topic and key number? If so, provide the full regional citation of the case according to Rule 10 of *The Bluebook*.

5.   Now you will use the topic approach. The topic approach merely involves reading the list of key numbers at the beginning of the topic (the topic outline) and looking for relevant key numbers. Go back to the topic outline (called "Analysis") for **Malicious Prosecution**. If you were looking for cases that discuss pleading the want of probable cause in an action, under what topic and key number would you look?

6.   Look up that key number. State the name of the 1958 Wisconsin Supreme Court case listed.

7.   Now you will use the subject approach. Look in the Descriptive Word Index volumes (either at the beginning or the end of the set). Using the descriptive word approach, find the topic and key number for cases concerning exemplary damages in malicious prosecution actions. To what topic and key number are you referred?

8.   Look up the topic and key number and find the 1963 Wisconsin Supreme Court case. List the full regional citation of the case in correct form.

SECTION I: Complete Questions 9a-13a in Section I if you used a state or regional digest for this assignment.

HOW TO UPDATE YOUR DIGEST RESEARCH IF YOU ARE USING A STATE OR REGIONAL DIGEST

Step 1. Current digest volumes are supplemented by annual pocket parts. Look in the pocket part for your topic and key number.

OR

If the pocket part is too thick to fit in the volume, the pocket part becomes a free standing pamphlet that updates that particular volume. Look in the pamphlet for your topic and key number.

Step 2. Depending on how recently the annual pocket parts were issued, your digest may have a pamphlet that directly supplements the annual pocket parts. If so, look up your topic and key number in this pamphlet.

Step 3. If the digest has a supplemental pamphlet from Step 2, check the "Closing with Cases Reported in" section on the second page of the pamphlet. If there is not a supplemental pamphlet, check the "Closing with Cases Reported in" section on the second page of the pocket part/pamphlet from Step 1.

Step 4. Go the reporter volume that you identified in Step 3. Beginning with the volume listed in the "Closing with Cases Reported in" from Step 3, look in the digest sections in the back of all bound volumes and in the front of all advance sheets to see if any recent cases have appeared under your topic and key number.

9a. Does your digest volume have a pocket part or pamphlet as explained in Step 1? If so, look up the topic and key number from Question 7. Are there any cases from Wisconsin digested under this topic and key number?

10a. Does your digest have a supplemental pamphlet as explained in Step 2? If so, look up the topic and key number from Question 7. Are there any cases from Wisconsin digested under this topic and key number?

11a.   Perform Step 3 of updating the digest by looking at the "Closing with Cases Reported in" statement on the second page of the supplemental pamphlet for the digest if there are any. If not, look at the "Closing with Cases Reported in" on the second page of the pocket part/pamphlet. According to the "Closing with Cases Reported in," what is the last volume of N.W.2d that the digest pocket part/pamphlet covers?

Now go to the *North Western Reporter 2d* and find the volume from Question 11a.

12a.   Each bound reporter volume has a small digest section in the back which gives you the topics and key numbers for the cases printed in that volume. Normally, you would check the digest sections of all of the bound reporters beginning with the volume from Question 11a. For this assignment, however, check **only** the **most recent** bound volume. Are there any Wisconsin cases digested under your topic and key number?

13a.   Now check the *North Western Reporter's* advance sheets. Bound volumes are updated by paperbound advance sheets. Several advance sheets are bound together into a reporter. In advance sheets, the digest section is in the front, just before the decisions begin. Normally, you would look at the digest section in all of the advance sheets for your topic and key number. For this assignment, however, check **only** the **most recent** advance sheet. Are there any Wisconsin cases are digested under your topic and key number?

SECTION II: Complete Questions 9b-13b in Section II if you used a Decennial Digest for this assignment.

   HOW TO UPDATE YOUR DIGEST RESEARCH IF YOU ARE USING A DECENNIAL DIGEST:

Step 1. **Look for your topic and key number in all of the subsequent Decennial Digests that were issued after the one you used in this assignment.**

Step 2. **The most recent Decennial Digest is updated by the General Digest. You will need to look at every volume of the General Digest for your topic and key number.**

Step 3. Check the "Closing with Cases Reported in" on the second page of the last General Digest on the shelf.

Step 4. Go the reporter volume that you identified in Step 3. Beginning with the volume listed in the "Closing with Cases Reported in" from Step 3, look in the digest sections in the back of all bound volumes and in the front of all advance sheets to see if any recent cases have appeared under your topic and key number.

9b.   Are there any subsequent Decennial Digests since the Decennial Digest you used in this exercise? If so, look up the topic and key number from Question 7 in each subsequent Decennial Digest. Are there any cases from Wisconsin digested under this topic and key number?

10b.   Find the General Digests. Look up the topic and key number from Question 7 in each volume of the General Digest. Are there any cases from Wisconsin digested under this topic and key number?

11b.   Perform Step 3 of updating the digest by looking at the "Closing with Cases Reported in" statement on the second page of the last General Digest on the shelf. According to the "Closing with Cases Reported in," what is the last volume of N.W.2d that this volume of the General Digest covers?

Now go to the *North Western Reporter 2d* and find the volume from Question 11b.

12b.   Each bound reporter volume has a small digest section in the back which gives you the topics and key numbers for the cases printed in that volume. Normally, you would check the digest sections of all of the bound reporters beginning with the volume from Question 11b. For this assignment, however, check **only** the **most recent** bound volume. Are there any Wisconsin cases digested under your topic and key number?

13b.   Now check the *North Western Reporter's* advance sheets. Bound volumes are updated by paperbound advance sheets. Several advance sheets are bound together into a reporter. In advance sheets, the digest section is in the front, just before the decisions begin. Normally, you would look at the digest section in all of the advance sheets for your topic and key number. For this assignment, however, check **only** the **most recent** advance sheet. Are there any Wisconsin cases digested under your topic and key number?

One great advantage of the West topic and key number system is that you can use it for **all jurisdictions**. The same topic and key number can be used for researching all state and federal courts whose decisions are published in West reporters. Different West digests will group jurisdictions in different ways. For example, the *Kansas Digest* contains Kansas cases and federal cases arising in Kansas. Each West state digest has similar coverage.

Regional digests contain state cases from each state covered by that particular region. The federal digests cover all of the federal courts, and the Decennial and General Digests, all of the state and federal jurisdictions. Use the most appropriate digest in your library, and provide the full citation, in correct form, for the following cases. Search under the topic and key number from **Question 2**.

14.   Check the *Colorado Digest 2d*, the *Pacific Digest* (Beginning 367 P.2d), or the *Seventh Decennial Digest*. Provide the full regional citation, in correct form, of the 1965 Colorado Supreme Court case digested under the topic and key number from Question 2.

15.   Check the *Federal Practice Digest 4th*. Is there a 1994 Eleventh Circuit Court of Appeals case arising from Georgia digested under this topic and key number? If so, provide the full citation in correct form.

ASSIGNMENT FOUR
FINDING CASES–DIGESTS
EXERCISE C

GOALS OF THIS ASSIGNMENT:
To introduce you to West digests.
To give you practice at the various methods of using digests.

CITATION RULES: For this assignment when citing a case, assume you are citing the case in a legal document that will be submitted to a state court that does not require parallel cites.

Please research Georgia cases to find cases dealing with the proper venue in actions by or against foreign corporations. Another attorney has given you a relevant case, *Orkin Exterminating Co. v. Morrison*, a 1988 Court of Appeals of Georgia case which has a headnote on point. Use this case to find other relevant cases. This is called the "one good case" approach. Check the Table of Cases in either 1) the *Georgia Digest 2d*; 2) the *South Eastern Digest 2d*; or 3) the *Tenth Decennial Digest, Part 1* (in that order of preference) to find the regional cite for the case.

1.   What is the regional cite for the case?

2.   Look up the case in the regional reporter. The relevant headnotes for our issue are headnotes two, three and four. What is the West topic and key number of headnote two?

3.   We now have a West topic and key number to begin our digest research. First, let's find out just what this topic and key number represent. Find the analysis outline at the very beginning of the topic from Question 2 in your digest. Examine the list of key numbers. What does the key number from Question 2 stand for? Include all relevant topics of which your key number may be a subtopic.

You will be using the same digest to answer Questions 4-11a or 4-11b.

4.   Go to your key number and look at the cases listed under it. Is there a Georgia Court of Appeals case from 1990 digested under this topic and key number? If so, provide the full regional citation of the case according to Rule 10 of *The Bluebook.*

5.   Now you will use the topic approach. The topic approach merely involves reading the list of key numbers at the beginning of the topic (the topic outline) and looking for relevant key numbers. Go back to the topic outline (called "Analysis") for **Corporations**. If you were looking for cases concerning foreign corporations obtaining a license or certificate, under what topic and key number would you look?

6.   Look up that key number. State the name of the 1990 Georgia Court of Appeals case listed.

7.   Now you will use the subject approach. Look in the Descriptive Word Index volumes (either at the beginning or the end of the set). Using the descriptive word approach, find the topic and key number for cases dealing with a foreign corporation's right to sue or defend as affected by or depending on compliance with statutory requirements in general. To what topic and key number are you referred?

8.   Look up the topic and key number and find a 1989 Georgia Court of Appeals case. List the full regional citation of the case in correct form.

SECTION I: Complete Questions 9a-13a in Section I if you used a state or regional digest for this assignment.

HOW TO UPDATE YOUR DIGEST RESEARCH IF YOU ARE USING A STATE OR REGIONAL DIGEST

Step 1. Current digest volumes are supplemented by annual pocket parts. Look in the pocket part for your topic and key number.
> **OR**

If the pocket part is too thick to fit in the volume, the pocket part becomes a free standing pamphlet that updates that particular volume. Look in the pamphlet for your topic and key number.

Step 2. Depending on how recently the annual pocket parts were issued, your digest may have a pamphlet that directly supplements the annual pocket parts. If so, look up your topic and key number in this pamphlet.

Step 3. If the digest has a supplemental pamphlet from Step 2, check the "Closing with Cases Reported in" section on the second page of the pamphlet. If there is not a supplemental pamphlet, check the "Closing with Cases Reported in" section on the second page of the pocket part/pamphlet from Step 1.

Step 4. Go the reporter volume that you identified in Step 3. Beginning with the volume listed in the "Closing with Cases Reported in" from Step 3, look in the digest sections in the back of all bound volumes and in the front of all advance sheets to see if any recent cases have appeared under your topic and key number.

9a. Does your digest volume have a pocket part or pamphlet as explained in Step 1? If so, look up the topic and key number from Question 7. Are there any cases from Georgia digested under this topic and key number?

10a. Does your digest have a supplemental pamphlet as explained in Step 2? If so, look up the topic and key number from Question 7. Are there any cases from Georgia digested under this topic and key number?

11a.   Perform Step 3 of updating the digest by looking at the "Closing with Cases Reported in" statement on the second page of the supplemental pamphlet for the digest if there are any. If not, look at the "Closing with Cases Reported in" on the second page of the pocket part/pamphlet. According to the "Closing with Cases Reported in," what is the last volume of S.E.2d that the digest pocket part/pamphlet covers?

Now go to the *South Eastern Reporter 2d* and find the volume from Question 11a.

12a.   Each bound reporter volume has a small digest section in the back which gives you the topics and key numbers for the cases printed in that volume. Normally, you would check the digest sections of all of the bound reporters beginning with the volume from Question 11a. For this assignment, however, check **only** the **most recent** bound volume. Are there any Georgia cases digested under your topic and key number?

13a.   Now check the *South Eastern Reporter's* advance sheets. Bound volumes are updated by paperbound advance sheets. Several advance sheets are bound together into a reporter. In advance sheets, the digest section is in the front, just before the decisions begin. Normally, you would look at the digest section in all of the advance sheets for your topic and key number. For this assignment, however, check **only** the **most recent** advance sheet. Are there any Georgia cases are digested under your topic and key number?

SECTION II: Complete Questions 9b-13b in Section II if you used a Decennial Digest for this assignment.

HOW TO UPDATE YOUR DIGEST RESEARCH IF YOU ARE USING A DECENNIAL DIGEST:

Step 1. Look for your topic and key number in all of the subsequent Decennial Digests that were issued after the one you used in this assignment.

Step 2. The most recent Decennial Digest is updated by the General Digest. You will need to look at every volume of the General Digest for your topic and key number.

Step 3. Check the "Closing with Cases Reported in" on the second page of the last General Digest on the shelf.

Step 4. Go the reporter volume that you identified in Step 3. Beginning with the volume listed in the "Closing with Cases Reported in" from Step 3, look in the digest sections in the back of all bound volumes and in the front of all advance sheets to see if any recent cases have appeared under your topic and key number.

9b.   Are there any subsequent Decennial Digests since the Decennial Digest you used in this exercise? If so, look up the topic and key number from Question 7 in each subsequent Decennial Digest. Are there any cases from Georgia digested under this topic and key number?

10b.   Find the General Digests. Look up the topic and key number from Question 7 in each volume of the General Digest. Are there any cases from Georgia digested under this topic and key number?

11b.   Perform Step 3 of updating the digest by looking at the "Closing with Cases Reported in" statement on the second page of the last General Digest on the shelf. According to the "Closing with Cases Reported in," what is the last volume of S.E.2d that this volume of the General Digest covers?

Now go to the *South Eastern Reporter 2d* and find the volume from Question 11b.

12b.   Each bound reporter volume has a small digest section in the back which gives you the topics and key numbers for the cases printed in that volume. Normally, you would check the digest sections of all of the bound reporters beginning with the volume from Question 11b. For this assignment, however, check **only** the **most recent** bound volume. Are there any Georgia cases digested under your topic and key number?

13b.   Now check the *South Eastern Reporter's* advance sheets. Bound volumes are updated by paperbound advance sheets. Several advance sheets are bound together into a reporter. In advance sheets, the digest section is in the front, just before the decisions begin. Normally, you would look at the digest section in all of the advance sheets for your topic and key number. For this assignment, however, check **only** the **most recent** advance sheet. Are there any Georgia cases digested under your topic and key number?

One great advantage of the West topic and key number system is that you can use it for **all jurisdictions**. The same topic and key number can be used for researching all state and federal courts whose decisions are published in West reporters. Different West digests will group jurisdictions in different ways. For example, the *Kansas Digest* contains Kansas cases and federal cases arising in Kansas. Each West state digest has similar coverage.

Regional digests contain state cases from each state covered by that particular region. The federal digests cover all of the federal courts, and the Decennial and General Digests, all of the state and federal jurisdictions. Use the most appropriate digest in your library, and provide the full citation, in correct form, for the following cases. Search under the topic and key number from **Question 2**.

14.   Check the *Iowa Digest*, the *North Western Digest 2d*, or the *Tenth Decennial Digest, Part 1*. Provide the full regional citation, in correct form, of the 1990 Iowa Supreme Court case digested under the topic and key number from Question 2.

15.   Check the *Federal Practice Digest 4th*. Is there a 1990 federal district court case arising from Illinois digested under this topic and key number? If so, provide the full citation in correct form omitting subsequent history.

ASSIGNMENT FOUR
FINDING CASES–DIGESTS
EXERCISE D

GOALS OF THIS ASSIGNMENT:
To introduce you to West digests.
To give you practice at the various methods of using digests.

CITATION RULES: For this assignment when citing a case, assume you are citing the case in a legal document that will be submitted to a state court that does not require parallel cites.

Please research New Jersey workers' compensation cases to determine if the control test for deciding whether a claimant is an employee or an independent contractor is fulfilled if the employer had a right of control over the worker even though actual control was not exercised. Another attorney has given you a relevant case, *Kertesz v. Korsh*, a 1996 Superior Court of New Jersey, Appellate Division case which has a headnote on point. Use this case to find other relevant cases. This is called the "one good case" approach. Check the Table of Cases in either 1) the *New Jersey Digest 2d*; 2) the *Atlantic Digest 2d*; or 3) the *Eleventh Decennial Digest, Part 1* (in that order of preference) to find the regional cite for the case. **Remember: Recent cases are found in the pocket parts of the state and regional digest.**

1.   What is the regional cite for the case?

2.   Look up the case in the regional reporter. The relevant headnote for our issue is headnotes seven. What is the West topic and key number of headnote seven?

3.   We now have a West topic and key number to begin our digest research. First, let's find out just what this topic and key number represent. Find the analysis outline at the very beginning of the topic from Question 2 in your digest. Examine the list of key numbers. What does the key number from Question 2 stand for? Include all relevant topics of which your key number may be a subtopic.

You will be using the same digest to answer Questions 4-11a or 4-11b.

4.   Go to your key number and look at the cases listed under it. Is there a Superior Court of New Jersey, Appellate Division case from 1997 digested under this topic and key number? If so, provide the full regional citation of the case according to Rule 10 of *The Bluebook*.

5.   Now you will use the topic approach. The topic approach merely involves reading the list of key numbers at the beginning of the topic (the topic outline) and looking for relevant key numbers. Go back to the topic outline (called "Analysis") for **Workers' Compensation**. If you were looking for cases discussing whether independent contractors in general are employees who fall within the Workmen's Compensation Acts, under what topic and key number would you look?

6.   Look up that key number. State the name of the 1998 Superior Court of New Jersey, Appellate Division case listed.

7.   Now you will use the subject approach. Look in the Descriptive Word Index volumes (either at the beginning or the end of the set). Using the descriptive word approach, find the topic and key number relating to the definitions of employees covered by compensation acts in workers' compensation cases. To what topic and key number are you referred?

8.   Look up the topic and key number and find a 1998 Superior Court of New Jersey, Appellate Division case. List the full regional citation of the case in correct form.

SECTION I: Complete Questions 9a-13a in Section I if you used a state or regional digest for this assignment.

HOW TO UPDATE YOUR DIGEST RESEARCH IF YOU ARE USING A STATE OR REGIONAL DIGEST

Step 1. Current digest volumes are supplemented by annual pocket parts. Look in the pocket part for your topic and key number.
>   **OR**
>
> If the pocket part is too thick to fit in the volume, the pocket part becomes a free standing pamphlet that updates that particular volume. Look in the pamphlet for your topic and key number.

Step 2. Depending on how recently the annual pocket parts were issued, your digest may have a pamphlet that directly supplements the annual pocket parts. If so, look up your topic and key number in this pamphlet.

Step 3. If the digest has a supplemental pamphlet from Step 2, check the "Closing with Cases Reported in" section on the second page of the pamphlet. If there is not a supplemental pamphlet, check the "Closing with Cases Reported in" section on the second page of the pocket part/pamphlet from Step 1.

Step 4. Go the reporter volume that you identified in Step 3. Beginning with the volume listed in the "Closing with Cases Reported in" from Step 3, look in the digest sections in the back of all bound volumes and in the front of all advance sheets to see if any recent cases have appeared under your topic and key number.

9a.   Does your digest volume have a pocket part or pamphlet as explained in Step 1? If so, look up the topic and key number from Question 7. Are there any cases from New Jersey digested under this topic and key number?

10a.   Does your digest have a supplemental pamphlet as explained in Step 2? If so, look up the topic and key number from Question 7. Are there any cases from New Jersey digested under this topic and key number?

11a. Perform Step 3 of updating the digest by looking at the "Closing with Cases Reported in" statement on the second page of the supplemental pamphlet for the digest if there are any. If not, look at the "Closing with Cases Reported in" on the second page of the pocket part/pamphlet. According to the "Closing with Cases Reported in," what is the last volume of A.2d that the digest pocket part/pamphlet covers?

Now go to the *Atlantic Reporter 2d* and find the volume from Question 11a.

12a. Each bound reporter volume has a small digest section in the back which gives you the topics and key numbers for the cases printed in that volume. Normally, you would check the digest sections of all of the bound reporters beginning with the volume from Question 11a. For this assignment, however, check **only** the **most recent** bound volume. Are there any New Jersey cases digested under your topic and key number?

13a. Now check the *Atlantic Reporter's* advance sheets. Bound volumes are updated by paperbound advance sheets. Several advance sheets are bound together into a reporter. In advance sheets, the digest section is in the front, just before the decisions begin. Normally, you would look at the digest section in all of the advance sheets for your topic and key number. For this assignment, however, check **only** the **most recent** advance sheet. Are there any New Jersey cases are digested under your topic and key number?

SECTION II: Complete Questions 9b-13b in Section II if you used a Decennial Digest for this assignment.

HOW TO UPDATE YOUR DIGEST RESEARCH IF YOU ARE USING A DECENNIAL DIGEST:

Step 1. Look for your topic and key number in all of the subsequent Decennial Digests that were issued after the one you used in this assignment.

Step 2. The most recent Decennial Digest is updated by the General Digest. You will need to look at every volume of the General Digest for your topic and key number.

Step 3. Check the "Closing with Cases Reported in" on the second page of the last General Digest on the shelf.

Step 4. Go the reporter volume that you identified in Step 3. Beginning with the volume listed in the "Closing with Cases Reported in" from Step 3, look in the digest sections in the back of all bound volumes and in the front of all advance sheets to see if any recent cases have appeared under your topic and key number.

9b.   Are there any subsequent Decennial Digests since the Decennial Digest you used in this exercise? If so, look up the topic and key number from Question 7 in each subsequent Decennial Digest. Are there any cases from New Jersey digested under this topic and key number?

10b.   Find the General Digests. Look up the topic and key number from Question 7 in each volume of the General Digest. Are there any cases from New Jersey digested under this topic and key number?

11b.   Perform Step 3 of updating the digest by looking at the "Closing with Cases Reported in" statement on the second page of the last General Digest on the shelf. According to the "Closing with Cases Reported in," what is the last volume of A.2d that this volume of the General Digest covers?

Now go to the *Atlantic Reporter 2d* and find the volume from Question 11b.

12b.   Each bound reporter volume has a small digest section in the back which gives you the topics and key numbers for the cases printed in that volume. Normally, you would check the digest sections of all of the bound reporters beginning with the volume from Question 11b. For this assignment, however, check **only** the **most recent** bound volume. Are there any New Jersey cases digested under your topic and key number?

13b. Now check the *Atlantic Reporter's* advance sheets. Bound volumes are updated by paperbound advance sheets. Several advance sheets are bound together into a reporter. In advance sheets, the digest section is in the front, just before the decisions begin. Normally, you would look at the digest section in all of the advance sheets for your topic and key number. For this assignment, however, check **only** the **most recent** advance sheet. Are there any New Jersey cases digested under your topic and key number?

One great advantage of the West topic and key number system is that you can use it for **all jurisdictions**. The same topic and key number can be used for researching all state and federal courts whose decisions are published in West reporters. Different West digests will group jurisdictions in different ways. For example, the *Kansas Digest* contains Kansas cases and federal cases arising in Kansas. Each West state digest has similar coverage.

Regional digests contain state cases from each state covered by that particular region. The federal digests cover all of the federal courts, and the Decennial and General Digests, all of the state and federal jurisdictions. Use the most appropriate digest in your library, and provide the full citation, in correct form, for the following cases. Search under the topic and key number from **Question 2. Hint: Make sure you check the pocket parts for more recent cases.**

14. Check the *South Carolina Digest*, the *South Eastern Digest 2d*, or the *Eleventh Decennial Digest, Part 1*. Provide the full regional citation, in correct form, of the 2000 South Carolina Supreme Court case digested under the topic and key number from Question 2.

15. Check the *Federal Practice Digest 4th*. Is there a 2000 federal district court case arising out of Pennsylvania digested under this topic and key number? If so, provide the full citation in correct form without providing subsequent history.

ASSIGNMENT FIVE
UPDATING AND VALIDATING CASES–CITATORS
EXERCISE A

GOAL OF THIS ASSIGNMENT:
To teach you how to identify a parallel cite, case history, and case treatment in a
<u>**Shepard's entry either in paper or in Shepard's online and Westlaw's KeyCite.**</u>

> **You are researching Kansas law for a trial brief you are writing. The subject of the brief**
> **is corporate law, particularly actions involving shareholders of corporations and matters**
> **of stock. You have found several cases that you would like to use in your brief but first**
> **need to update the cases to verify they are still good law.**

SECTION I: Complete Questions 1a-14a in Section I if your library has the Shepard's volumes
available in print.

> CITATION RULES: When a case cite appears in your answers, use the standard abbreviation
> for the reporter as found in *The Bluebook: A Uniform System of Citation*, 18th ed. It may differ
> substantially from the Shepard's abbreviation. Do not include the case name in your answers.

> **In questions 1a-4a, Shepardize *Hotchkiss v. Fischer*, 16 P.2d 531 (Kan. 1932). Find the**
> **case in the <u>bound</u> *Shepard's Pacific Citations* volumes that contain cites to it.**

1a.   Shepardize the case. What is its parallel cite to the official reporter?

2a.   Has an Idaho case cited the *Hotchkiss* case? If so, state its regional cite as listed in Shepard's.
        Remember, Shepard's in print does not list the first page of the case, but only the actual page
        that cites your case.

3a.   What is the regional cite of the decision that distinguished the *Hotchkiss* case?

4a.   Has an A.L.R.3d annotation cited *Hotchkiss*? If so, state the cite.

Reshelve Shepard's Citations.

5a.   Look up the case in your answer to Question 2. Does this case deal with the issue of corporate stock ?

Now, you will Shepardize a U.S. Supreme Court case *Blau v. Lehman*, 368 U.S. 403, 82 S. Ct. 451, 7 L. Ed. 2d 403. Examine the spine of *Shepard's United States Citations–Case Edition*, Volumes 1.1 - 1.11 and find the volume in which your case appears to answer Questions 6a - 14a.

6a.   How does Shepard's show parallel cites?

7a.   What is the cite of the same case in federal district court?

8a.   What is the cite of the court of appeals case from the Third Circuit that explained the *Blau* case?

9a.   What is the regional cite of the Mississippi decision that cited the *Blau* case?

10a.   What Eighth Circuit court of appeals case's dissent cited *Blau*?

11a.   State the Shepard's entry for the A.L.R.2d annotation that cited *Blau*.

12a.   Did the A.L.R. reference in the previous question appear in the annotation or its supplement? If you need help with this question, refer to the preface

13a.   If your *Shepard's United States Citations–Case Edition* includes volumes covering L. Ed. cites, find the listing for 368 U.S. 403 under its L. Ed. 2d cite. What is the cite of the district court case from the First Circuit that cited *Blau* for the issue of law covered by the sixth headnote?

14a.   If your set includes volumes covering S. Ct. cites, find the listings for 368 U.S. 403 under its S. Ct. cite. What court of appeals opinion from the Fifth Circuit cited a point of law from West headnote number 1 of your case?

SECTION II: Complete the Questions 1b-13b in section II, if your library does NOT have the Shepard's volumes in print. Use Shepard's online for Questions 1b-6b and Westlaw's KeyCite service for Questions 7b-13b.

CITATION RULES: When a case cite appears in your answers, use the standard abbreviation for the reporter as found in *The Bluebook: A Uniform System of Citation*, 18th ed., give the first page of the citing case, and give the pinpoint cite to the page on which the case you are Shepardizing is cited. Do not include the case name in your answers.

In questions 1b-6b, Shepardize *Hotchkiss v. Fischer*, 16 P.2d 531 (Kan. 1932). Logon to http://www.lexisnexis.com/shepards/ or http://www.lexisnexis.com/lawschool/.

1b.   Shepardize the case. What is its parallel cite to the official reporter?

2b.   Has a 1956 Texas case cited the *Hotchkiss* case? If so, state its regional cite.

3b.   Click on the link to the case in your answer to Question 2. Does this case deal with the issue of corporate stock?

4b.   What is the regional cite of the 1934 decision that distinguished the *Hotchkiss* case?

5b.   Has an A.L.R.3d annotation cited *Hotchkiss*? If so, state the cite.

Custom Restrictions in Shepard's online allows you to limit your citing references by analysis, jurisdiction, headnote and date. Use the Custom link to help you find the following case:

6b.   What is the cite of the 1981 court of appeals case from the 10th Circuit that cited *Hotchkiss* for the issue of law covered by the third headnote in th P.2d version of the *Hotchkiss* case?

Logoff Shepard's.

Now, you will use Westlaw's KeyCite service to update the case *Blau v. Lehman*, 368 U.S. 403. Logon to Westlaw at http://lawschool.westlaw.com.

7b.   What are the parallel cites to *West's Supreme Court Reporter* and *U.S. Supreme Court Reports, Lawyers' Edition*?

8b.   In the direct history, what is the cite of the same case in the federal district court?

9b.   What is the cite of the 1981 court of appeals case from the Ninth Circuit that distinguished the *Blau* case?

10b.   What is the cite of the 1969 Second Circuit Court of Appeals decision that examined (four star treatment) the *Blau* case?

11b.   What 2001 United States Supreme Court case's dissent cited (two star treatment) *Blau*? Provide the U.S. Reports cite.

The Limit KeyCite Display allows you to limit your citing references by headnotes, jurisdiction, date, document type, and depth of treatment. Use Limit KeyCite Display to answer the following questions:

12b.   State the name of the 86 A.L.R. Fed. annotation that cited *Blau*.

13b.   What 1970 Seventh Circuit Court of Appeals case mentioned (one star treatment) a point of law from *West's Supreme Court Reporter* headnote number 6 (topic corporations) of your case?

Logoff Westlaw.

ASSIGNMENT FIVE
UPDATING AND VALIDATING CASES–CITATORS
EXERCISE B

GOAL OF THIS ASSIGNMENT:
To teach you how to identify a parallel cite, case history, and case treatment in a Shepard's entry either in paper or in Shepard's online and Westlaw's KeyCite.

You are researching Wisconsin law for a trial brief you are writing. The subject of the brief is malicious prosecution and abuse of process. You have found several cases that you would like to use in your brief but first need to update the cases to verify they are still good law.

SECTION I: Complete Questions 1a-14a in Section I if your library has the Shepard's volumes available in print.

CITATION RULES: When a case cite appears in your answers, use the standard abbreviation for the reporter as found in *The Bluebook: A Uniform System of Citation*, 18th ed. It may differ substantially from the Shepard's abbreviation. Do not include the case name in your answers.

In questions 1a-4a, Shepardize *Strid v. Converse*, 331 N.W.2d 350 (Wis. 1983). Find the case in the bound *Shepard's Northwestern Citations* volumes that contain cites to it.

1a.   Shepardize the case. What is its parallel cite to the official reporter?

2a.   Has a South Dakota case cited the *Strid* case? If so, state its regional cite as listed in Shepard's. Remember, Shepard's in print does not list the first page of the case, but only the actual page that cites your case.

3a.   What is the regional cite of the decision that distinguished the *Strid* case?

4a.   Have any A.L.R.4th annotations cited *Strid*? If so, state the cite.

Reshelve Shepard's Citations.

5a.   Look up the case in your answer to Question 2. Does this case concern malicious prosecution or abuse of process?

Now, you will Shepardize a U.S. Supreme Court case *Imbler v. Pachtman*, 424 U.S. 409, 96 S. Ct. 984, 47 L. Ed. 2d 128. Examine the spine of *Shepard's United States Citations–Case Edition*, Volumes 1.1 - 1.11 and find the volume in which your case appears to answer Questions 6a - 14a.

6a.   How does Shepard's show parallel cites?

7a.   What is the cite of the same case in federal appellate court?

8a.   What is the cite of the **first listed** court of appeals case from the First Circuit that explained the *Imbler* case?

9a.   What is the regional cite of the **first listed** Alaska decision that cited *Imbler*?

10a.   What **first listed** Second Circuit court of appeals case's dissent cited *Imbler*?

11a.   State the Shepard's entry for the A.L.R.4th annotation that cited *Imbler*.

12a.   Did the A.L.R. reference in the previous question appear in the annotation or its supplement? If you need help with this question, refer to the preface.

13a.   If your *Shepard's United States Citations–Case Edition* includes volumes covering L. Ed. cites, find the listing for 424 U.S. 409 under its L. Ed. 2d cite. What is the cite of the **first listed** court of appeals case from the First Circuit that cited *Imbler* for the issue of law covered by the fifth headnote?

14a.   If your set includes volumes covering S. Ct. cites, find the listings for 424 U.S. 409 under its S. Ct. cite. What is the cite of the **first listed** court of appeals case from the Second Circuit that cited a point of law from West headnote number 5 of your case?

SECTION II: Complete the Questions 1b-13b in section II, if your library does NOT have the Shepard's volumes in print. Use Shepard's online for Questions 1b-6b and Westlaw's KeyCite service for Questions 7b-13b.

CITATION RULES: When a case cite appears in your answers, use the standard abbreviation for the reporter as found in *The Bluebook: A Uniform System of Citation*, 18th ed., give the first page of the citing case, and give the pinpoint cite to the page on which the case you are Shepardizing is cited. Do not include the case name in your answers.

Questions 1b-6b require you to Shepardize *Strid v. Converse*, 331 N.W.2d 350 (Wis. 1983). Logon to http://www.lexisnexis.com/shepards/ or http://www.lexisnexis.com/lawschool.

1b.   Shepardize the case. What is its parallel cite to the official reporter?

2b.   Has a 1993 Alabama case cited the *Strid* case? If so, state its regional cite.

3b.   Click on the link to the case in your answer to Question 2. Does this case concern malicious prosecution or abuse of process?

4b.   What is the regional 1991 cite of the decision that distinguished the *Strid* case?

5b.   Has an A.L.R.4th annotation cited *Strid*? If so, state the cite.

Custom Restrictions in Shepard's online allows you to limit your citing references by analysis, jurisdiction, headnote and date. Use Custom Restrictions to help you find the following case:

6b.   What is the cite of the 1998 court of appeals case from the 7th Circuit that cited *Strid* for the issue of law covered by the fourth headnote in th N.W.2d version of the *Strid* case?

Logoff Shepard's.

Now, you will use Westlaw's KeyCite service to update the case *Imbler v. Pachtman*, 424 U.S. 409. Logon to Westlaw at http://lawschool.westlaw.com.

7b.   What are the parallel cites to *West's Supreme Court Reporter* and *U.S. Supreme Court Reports, Lawyers' Edition*?

8b.   In the direct history, what is the cite of the same case in the federal appellate court?

9b.   What is the cite of the 1992 court of appeals case from the Seventh Circuit that declined to the *Imbler* case?

10b.   What is the cite of the 1989 Second Circuit Court of Appeals decision that examined (four star treatment) *Imbler*?

11b.   What 1994 United States Supreme Court case's dissent discussed (three star treatment) *Imbler*? Provide the U.S. Reports cite.

The Limit KeyCite Display allows you to limit your citing references by headnotes, jurisdiction, date, document type, and depth of treatment. Use Limit KeyCite Display to answer the following questions:

12b.   State the name of the A.L.R.4th annotation that cited *Imbler*.

13b.   What 1992 First Circuit Court of Appeals case examined (four star treatment) a point of law from *West's Supreme Court Reporter* headnote number 3 of your case?

Logoff Westlaw.

ASSIGNMENT FIVE
UPDATING AND VALIDATING CASES–CITATORS
EXERCISE C

GOAL OF THIS ASSIGNMENT:
To teach you how to identify a parallel cite, case history, and case treatment in a Shepard's entry either in paper or in Shepard's online and Westlaw's KeyCite.

You are researching Georgia law for a trial brief you are writing. The subject of the brief deals with venue and jurisdiction as to foreign corporations. You have found several cases that you would like to use in your brief but first need to update the cases to verify they are still good law.

SECTION I: Complete Questions 1a-14a in Section I if your library has the Shepard's volumes available in print.

CITATION RULES: When a case cite appears in your answers, use the standard abbreviation for the reporter as found in *The Bluebook: A Uniform System of Citation*, 18th ed. It may differ substantially from the Shepard's abbreviation. Do not include the case name in your answers.

In questions 1a-4a, Shepardize *Allied Finance Co. v. Prosser*, 119 S.E.2d 813 (Ga. Ct. App. 1961). Find the case in the <u>bound</u> *Shepard's Southeastern Citations* volumes that contain cites to it.

1a.   Shepardize the case. What is its parallel cite to the official reporter?

2a.   Has an Ohio case cited the *Allied Finance* case? If so, state its regional cite as listed in Shepard's. Remember, Shepard's in print does not list the first page of the case, but only the actual page that cites your case.

3a.   What is the **first listed** regional cite of the decision that distinguished *Allied Finance*?

4a.   Has an A.L.R.3d annotation cited *Allied Finance*? If so, state the **fifth listed** cite.

Reshelve Shepard's Citations.

5a.   Look up the case in your answer to Question 2. Does this case involve a foreign corporation?

Now, you will Shepardize a U.S. Supreme Court case *Woods v. Interstate Realty Co.*, 337 U.S. 535, 69 S. Ct. 1235, 93 L. Ed. 1524. Examine the spine of *Shepard's United States Citations–Case Edition*, Volumes 1.1 - 1.11 and find the volume in which your case appears to answer Questions 6a - 14a.

6a.   How does Shepard's show parallel cites?

7a.   What is the **first listed** cite of the same case in federal appellate court?

8a.   What is the cite of the **first listed** court of appeals case from the Fifth Circuit that distinguished the *Woods* case?

9a.   What is the regional cite of the Alaska decision that cited the *Woods* case?

10a.   What Second Circuit court of appeals case's dissent cited *Woods*?

11a.   State the Shepard's entry for the A.L.R.2d annotation that cited *Woods*.

12a.   Did the A.L.R. reference in the previous question appear in the annotation or its supplement? If you need help with this question, refer to the preface.

13a.   If your *Shepard's United States Citations–Case Edition* includes volumes covering L. Ed. cites, find the listing for 337 U.S. 535 under its L. Ed. cite. What is the cite of the **first listed** court of appeals case from the Fourth Circuit that cited *Woods* for the issue of law covered by the third headnote?

14a.   If your set includes volumes covering S. Ct. cites, find the listings for the case from Question 6 under its S. Ct. cite. What court of appeals case from the Sixth Circuit cited a point of law from West headnote number 4 of your case?

SECTION II: Complete the Questions 1b-13b in section II, if your library does NOT have the Shepard's volumes in print. Use Shepard's online for Questions 1b-6b and Westlaw's KeyCite Service for Questions 7b-13b.

CITATION RULES: When a case cite appears in your answers, use the standard abbreviation for the reporter as found in *The Bluebook: A Uniform System of Citation*, 18th ed., give the first page of the citing case, and give the pinpoint cite to the page on which the case you are Shepardizing is cited. Do not include the case name in your answers.

In questions 1b-6b, Shepardize *Allied Finance Co. v. Prosser*, 119 S.E.2d 813 (Ga. Ct. App. 1961). Logon to http://www.lexisnexis.com/shepards/ or http://www.lexisnexis.com/lawschool.

1b.   Shepardize the case. What is its parallel cite to the official reporter?

2b.   Has a 1968 South Dakota case cited the *Allied Finance* case? If so, state its regional cite.

3b.   Click on the link to the case in your answer to Question 2. Does this case discuss the test of minimum contact to invoke personal jurisdiction over a nonresident individual or foreign corporation?

4b.   What is the regional cite of the **first listed** 1972 decision that distinguished the *Allied Finance* case?

5b.   Has an A.L.R.2d annotation cited *Allied Finance*? If so, state the cite.

Custom Restrictions in Shepard's online allows you to limit your citing references by analysis, jurisdiction, headnote and date. Use Custom Restrictions to help you find the following case:

6b.   What is the cite of the 1971 federal district court case from the Southern District of Georgia which is presently in the 11th Circuit that cited *Allied Finance* for the issue of law covered by the fourth headnote in th S.E.2d version of the *Allied Finance* case?

Logoff Shepard's.

Now, you will use Westlaw's KeyCite service to update the case *Woods v. Interstate Realty Co.*, 337 U.S. 535. Logon to Westlaw at http://lawschool.westlaw.com.

7b.   What are the parallel cites to *West's Supreme Court Reporter* and *U.S. Supreme Court Reports, Lawyers' Edition*?

8b.   In the direct history, what is the cite of the same case in the federal appellate court dated Nov. 26, 1948?

9b.   What is the cite of the 1964 court of appeals case from the Sixth Circuit that distinguished the *Woods* case?

10b.   What is the cite of the 1979 Third Circuit Court of Appeals decision that discussed (three star treatment) the *Woods* case?

11b.   What 1975 United States Supreme Court case's dissent cited (two star treatment) *Woods*? Provide the U.S. Reports cite.

The Limit KeyCite Display allows you to limit your citing references by headnotes, jurisdiction, date, document type, and depth of treatment. Use Limit KeyCite Display to answer the following questions:

12b.   State the name of the 26 A.L.R.3d annotation that cited *Woods*.

13b.   What 1974 Sixth Circuit Court of Appeals case discussed (three star treatment) a point of law from *West's Supreme Court Reporter* headnote number 4 of your case?

Logoff Westlaw.

ASSIGNMENT FIVE
UPDATING AND VALIDATING CASES–CITATORS
EXERCISE D

GOAL OF THIS ASSIGNMENT:
To teach you how to identify a parallel cite, case history, and case treatment in a Shepard's entry either in paper or in Shepard's online and Westlaw's KeyCite.

You are researching New Jersey law for a trial brief you are writing. The subject of the brief deals with workers' compensation. You have found several cases that you would like to use in your brief but first need to update the cases to verify they are still good law.

SECTION I: Complete Questions 1a-14a in Section I if your library has the Shepard's volumes available in print.

CITATION RULES: When a case cite appears in your answers, use the standard abbreviation for the reporter as found in *The Bluebook: A Uniform System of Citation*, 18th ed. It may differ substantially from the Shepard's abbreviation. Do not include the case name in your answers.

In questions 1a-4a, Shepardize *Kelly v. Hackensack Water Co.*, 77 A.2d 467 (N.J. Super. Ct. App. Div. 1950). Find the case in the bound *Shepard's Atlantic Citations* volumes that contain cites to it.

1a.   Shepardize the case. What is its parallel cite to the official reporter?

2a.   Has an Arkansas case cited the *Kelly* case? If so, state its regional cite as listed in Shepard's. Remember, Shepard's in print does not list the first page of the case, but only the actual page that cites your case.

3a.   What is the regional cite of the decision that distinguished the *Kelly* case?

4a.   Has an A.L.R.3d annotation cited *Kelly*? If so, state the **first listed** cite.

Reshelve Shepard's Citations.

5a.   Look up the case in your answer to Question 2. Does this case concern workers' compensation?

Now, you will Shepardize a U.S. Supreme Court case *Estate of Cowart v. Nicklos Drilling Co.*, 505 U.S. 469, 112 S. Ct. 2589, 120 L. Ed. 2d 379. Examine the spine of *Shepard's United States Citations–Case Edition*, Volumes 1.1 - 1.11 and find the volume in which your case appears to answer Questions 6a - 14a.

6a.   How does Shepard's show parallel cites?

7a.   What is the **first listed** cite of the same case in federal appellate court?

8a.   What is the cite of the court of appeals case from the Fourth Circuit that explained the *Estate of Cowart* case?

9a.   What is the regional cite of the Wyoming decision that cited the *Estate of Cowart* case?

10a.   What Ninth Circuit court of appeals case's dissent cited *Estate of Cowart*?

11a.   State the Shepard's entry for the A.L.R. Fed. annotation that cited *Estate of Cowart*.

12a.   Did the A.L.R. reference in the previous question appear in the annotation or its supplement? If you need help with this question, refer to the preface.

13a.   If your *Shepard's United States Citations–Case Edition* includes volumes covering L. Ed. cites, find the listing for 505 U.S. 469 under its L. Ed. 2d cite. What is the cite of the court of appeals case from the Third Circuit that cited *Estate of Cowart* for the issue of law covered by the first headnote?

14a.   If your set includes volumes covering S. Ct. cites, find the listings for the case from Question 6 under its S. Ct. cite. What court of appeals opinion from the Fourth   Circuit cited a point of law from West headnote number 7 of your case?

SECTION II: Complete the Questions 1b-13b in section II, if your library does NOT have the Shepard's volumes in print. Use Shepard's online for Questions 1b-6b and Westlaw's KeyCite service for Questions 7b-13b.

CITATION RULES: When a case cite appears in your answers, use the standard abbreviation for the reporter as found in *The Bluebook: A Uniform System of Citation*, 18th ed., give the first page of the citing case, and give the pinpoint cite to the page on which the case you are Shepardizing is cited. Do not include the case name your answers.

In questions 1b-6b, Shepardize *Kelly v. Hackensack Water Co.*, 77 A.2d 467 (N.J. Super. Ct. App. Div. 1950). Logon to http://www.lexisnexis.com/shepards/ or http://www.lexisnexis.com/lawschool.

1b.   Shepardize the case. What is its parallel cite to the official reporter?

2b.   Has a 1973 Michigan case cited the *Kelly* case? If so, state its regional cite.

3b.   Click on the link to the case in your answer to Question 2. Does this case concern workers' compensation?

4b.   What is the regional cite of the 1951 New Jersey Superior Court decision that distinguished the *Kelly* case?

5b.   Has an A.L.R.3d annotation cited *Kelly*? If so, state the cite.

Custom Restrictions in Shepard's online allows you to limit your citing references by analysis, jurisdiction, headnote and date. Use Custom Restrictions to help you find the following case:

6b.   What is the regional cite of the 1977 New Jersey Supreme Court case that cited *Kelly* for the issue of law covered by the fourth headnote in the A.2d version of the *Kelly* case?

Logoff Shepard's.

Now, you will use Westlaw's KeyCite service to update the case *Estate of Cowart v. Nicklos Drilling Co.*, 505 U.S. 469. Logon to Westlaw at http://lawschool.westlaw.com.

7b.   What are the parallel cites to *West's Supreme Court Reporter* and *U.S. Supreme Court Reports, Lawyers' Edition*?

8b.   In the direct history, what is the cite of the same case in the federal appellate court dated Aug. 9, 1990?

9b.   What is the cite of the 1997 court of appeals case from the Third Circuit that distinguished the *Estate of Cowart* case?

10b.   What is the cite of the 1997 Ninth Circuit Court of Appeals decision that examined (four star treatment) the *Estate of Cowart* case?

11b.   What 1996 United States Supreme Court case's dissent cited (two star treatment) *Estate of Cowart*? Provide the U.S. Reports cite.

The Limit KeyCite Display allows you to limit your citing references by headnotes, jurisdiction, date, document type, and depth of treatment. Use Limit KeyCite Display to answer the following questions:

12b.   State the name of the 26 A.L.R.3d annotation that cited *Estate of Cowart*.

13b.   What 1998 Fourth Circuit Court of Appeals case discussed (three star treatment) a point of law from *West's Supreme Court Reporter* headnote number 3 of your case?

Logoff Westlaw.

GOALS OF THIS ASSIGNMENT:
To give you practice at using the A.L.R. tables and indexes.
To find whether a relevant annotation has been superseded or supplemented.

> You are researching Kansas corporate law involving the duty and liability
> of majority stockholders to minority stockholders of the same closely-held
> corporation in obtaining stock of the minority shareholders. Use the Index
> to A.L.R. to find a relevant A.L.R.3d annotation by subject.

1.   What is the cite to the A.L.R.3d annotation?

Find the annotation from 7 A.L.R.3d and answer Questions 2-10.

2.   What is the correct citation of the annotation itself? (See Rule 16.6.6 of *The
       Bluebook*.) Hint: Older annotations list the author at the end of the annotation.

3.   Remember, the full text of an opinion precedes each annotation that explains the
       law in the case's subject area. State the full citation of the opinion whose text is
       printed in full.

4.   Go back to the annotation. To which sections of the Am. Jur. 2d topic
       Corporations could you turn to find related material?

5.   Examine the Index section. Which section discusses applicable provisions of the
       Securities and Exchange Act?

6. Examine the Table of Jurisdictions. This table will quickly tell you all jurisdictions covered by the annotation. Are any Kansas cases discussed in this annotation?

7. Examine the scope notes and the references to related matters in the preliminary matters. State the cite of the annotation listed which discusses the right of corporate officers to purchase corporate assets from the corporation.

8. Examine § 3. What 1932 Kansas case is cited in this section? State its name.

9. Look at the beginning of the annotation in the pocket part to this volume. Examine the beginning of the updating material for a note telling you that the annotation has been superseded. Is there a note telling you that this annotation has been superseded?

10. The pocket parts in A.L.R.3d, 4th, 5th and Fed. volumes also provide information on later cases that are relevant to the annotation. Provide the full regional citation of a 1996 Georgia Court of Appeals case that updates § 3 of the annotation.

Reshelve A.L.R. and find the last volume of the A.L.R. Index.

11. You can also tell if an annotation has been superseded by looking in the Annotation History Table, found at the end of the last A.L.R. Index volume and its pocket part. Has 57 A.L.R.2d 1351 been superseded? If so, state the cite of the superseding annotation.

ASSIGNMENT SIX
AMERICAN LAW REPORTS
EXERCISE B

GOALS OF THIS ASSIGNMENT:
To give you practice at using the A.L.R. tables and indexes.
To find whether a relevant annotation has been superseded or supplemented.

> **You are researching Wisconsin law involving liability for malicious prosecution of an attorney who is acting for her client. Use the Index to A.L.R. to find a relevant A.L.R.4th annotation by subject.**

1.   What is the cite to the A.L.R.4th annotation?

Find the annotation from 46 A.L.R.4th and answer Questions 2-10.

2.   What is the correct citation of the annotation itself? (See Rule 16.6.6 of *The Bluebook*.)

3.   Remember, the full text of an opinion accompanies each annotation that explains the law in the case's subject area. This case is referenced at the bottom of the first page of the annotation. State the full regional citation of the opinion whose text is printed in full.

4.   Go back to the annotation. To which sections of the Am. Jur. 2d topic *Malicious Prosecution* could you turn to find related material?

5.   Examine the Index section. Which section discusses knowledge of client's wrongdoing?

6.   Examine the Table of Jurisdictions. This table will quickly tell you all jurisdictions covered by the annotation. Are any Wisconsin cases discussed in this annotation?

7.   Examine the scope notes and the references to related matters in the preliminary matters. State the cite of the annotation listed which discusses the liability for malicious prosecution based on contest or caveat to will.

8.   Examine § 4[a]. What 1983 Wisconsin case is cited in this section? State its name.

9.   Look up the cite to the annotation in the pocket part to this volume. Examine the beginning of the updating material for a note telling you that the annotation has been superseded. Is there a note telling you that this annotation has been superseded?

10.   The pocket parts in A.L.R.3d, 4th, 5th and Fed. volumes also provide information on later cases that are relevant to the annotation. Provide the full regional citation of a 1992 Arizona case that updates § 4[a] of the annotation.

Reshelve A.L.R. and find the last volume of the A.L.R. Index.

11.   You can also tell if an annotation has been superseded by looking in the Annotation History Table, found at the end of the last A.L.R. Index volume and its pocket part. Has 48 A.L.R.3d 1271 been superseded? If so, state the cite of the superseding annotation.

ASSIGNMENT SIX
AMERICAN LAW REPORTS
EXERCISE C

GOALS OF THIS ASSIGNMENT:
To give you practice at using the A.L.R. tables and indexes.
To find whether a relevant annotation has been superseded or supplemented.

You are researching Georgia law involving foreign corporations whose casual and occasional acts result in a commission of a tort within a state, thus providing the state with in personam jurisdiction over the foreign corporation under the state statutes or rules of court. Use the Index to A.L.R. to find a relevant A.L.R.3d annotation by subject.

1.   What is the cite to the A.L.R.3d annotation?

Find the annotation from 24 A.L.R.3d and answer Questions 2-10.

2.   What is the correct citation of the annotation itself? (See Rule 16.6.6 of *The Bluebook*.) Hint: Older annotations list the author at the end of the annotation.

3.   Remember, the full text of an opinion precedes each annotation that explains the law in the case's subject area. State the full regional citation of the opinion whose text is printed in full.

4.   Go back to the annotation. To which section of the Am. Jur. 2d topic *Foreign Corporations* could you turn to find related material?

5.   Examine the Index section. Which section discusses conversion?

6.   Examine the Table of Jurisdictions. This table will quickly tell you all jurisdictions covered by the annotation. Are any Georgia cases discussed in this annotation?

7.   Examine the scope notes and the references to related matters in the prefatory matters. State the cite of the annotation listed which discusses foreign insurance company as subject to service of process in action on policy.

8.   Examine § 2[d]. What 1961 Georgia case is cited in this section? State its name.

9.   Look up the cite to the annotation in the pocket part to this volume. Examine the beginning of the updating material for a note telling you that the annotation has been superseded. Is there a note telling you that this annotation has been superseded?

10.   The pocket parts in A.L.R.3d, 4th, 5th and Fed. volumes also provide information on later cases that are relevant to the annotation. Provide the full regional citation of a 1983 federal district of Maryland case that updates § 2[d] of the annotation.

Reshelve A.L.R. and find the last volume of the A.L.R. Index.

11.   You can also tell if an annotation has been superseded by looking in the Annotation History Table, found at the end of the last A.L.R. Index volume and its pocket part. Has 51 A.L.R.4th 872 been superseded? If so, state the cite of the superseding annotation.

ASSIGNMENT SIX
AMERICAN LAW REPORTS
EXERCISE D

GOALS OF THIS ASSIGNMENT:
To give you practice at using the A.L.R. tables and indexes.
To find whether a relevant annotation has been superseded or supplemented.

You are researching New Jersey law involving workers' compensation for injury sustained while attending employer-sponsored social affair as arising out of and in the course of employment. Use the Index to A.L.R. to find a relevant A.L.R.3d annotation by subject.

1.   What is the cite to the A.L.R.3d annotation?

Find the annotation from 47 A.L.R.3d and answer Questions 2-10.

2.   What is the correct citation of the annotation itself? (See Rule 16.6.6 of *The Bluebook*.)

3.   Remember, the full text of an opinion precedes each annotation that explains the law in the case's subject area. State the full regional citation of the opinion whose text is printed in full.

4.   Go back to the annotation. To which sections of the Am. Jur. [1st edition] topic *Workmen's Compensation* could you turn to find related material?

5.   Examine the Index section. Which section discusses the encouragement by employer to attend the social affair?

6.   Examine the Table of Jurisdictions. This table will quickly tell you all jurisdictions covered by the annotation. Are any New Jersey cases discussed in this annotation?

7.   Examine the scope notes and the references to related matters in the preliminary matters. State the cite of the annotation listed which discusses the right of an employee to maintain a common-law action for negligence against workmen's compensation insurance carrier.

8.   Examine § 4. What 1950 New Jersey case is cited in this section? State its name.

9.   Look up the cite to the annotation in the pocket part to this volume. Examine the beginning of the updating material for a note telling you that the annotation has been superseded. Is there a note telling you that this annotation has been superseded?

10.   The pocket parts in A.L.R.3d, 4th, 5th and Fed. volumes also provide information on later cases that are relevant to the annotation. Provide the full regional citation of a 1986 Indiana case that updates § 4 of the annotation.

Reshelve A.L.R. and find the last volume of the A.L.R. Index.

11.   You can also tell if an annotation has been superseded by looking in the Annotation History Table, found at the end of the last A.L.R. Index volume and its pocket part. Has 86 A.L.R. Fed.782 been superseded? If so, state the cite of the superseding annotation.

ASSIGNMENT SEVEN
REVIEW--FINDING, CITING AND UPDATING CASES
EXERCISE A

GOALS OF THIS ASSIGNMENT:
To review the use of digests, citators in print or online and A.L.R. to find cases.
To combine several steps of a research strategy using different types of materials.

Yesterday, Dana Fellows, one of the partners in the criminal defense firm for which you are working as a summer associate in Albany, New York, asked you to help her research a situation that recently arose at the firm. Attorney Fellows related the facts to you. Two years ago, Fellows represented Michael R. in a federal criminal trial involving drug trafficking. The trial resulted in a not guilty verdict. Now, Mr. R.'s business partner Mr. D. has been arrested for racketeering. Mr. D. contacted Fellows and has asked her to be his attorney in the federal criminal trial in district court. Usually, a defendant has a right to retain the attorney of his choice providing there are no ethical impediments. However, it is a foregone conclusion that Mr. R. will be subpoenaed to testify against Mr. C. Attorney Fellows wants you to research federal cases in which the court has determined whether or not to **disqualify** the **defendant-chosen attorney** from representing the defendant in a **federal prosecution**. Please research federal case law to determine how the court may deal with this situation. Before you begin, identify the federal jurisdiction that includes New York and determine which courts' cases will be mandatory authority in that jurisdiction.

1.   If you are unfamiliar with a topic and looking for citations to primary authority for your jurisdiction, a good place to begin your research is in the A.L.R. Go to the A.L.R. Index and look for an A.L.R. Fed. annotation that may help you research this issue. What is the cite to the annotation?

Find the 127 A.L.R. Fed. annotation.

2.   What is the correct citation of the annotation itself? (See Rule 16.6.6 of *The Bluebook*.)

3.   In section 6[b], does this annotation provide you with a cite to a 1982 United States Court of Appeals Second Circuit arising out of New York case? If so, provide the full citation in correct format.

        Find the case from Question 3 and read it.

4.   Given your fact situation, is this case on point?

5.   Assuming your case will take place in a federal district court in New York, is this case mandatory authority?

6.   Look at the headnotes of this case. Several headnotes are relevant to your issue. Which headnote discusses the government's interest in preserving the integrity of the criminal proceeding by seeking to disqualify defense counsel whose former client was a potential witness? List its number, e.g., first, second, third, etc.

7.   What is the topic and key number of this headnote?

8.   Read the opinion corresponding to the point of law for the above headnote. According to this opinion, what was the name of the principal criminal case relied on by the government and the district court?

9.   Use *West's Federal Practice Digest 4th* to find other cases that are mandatory authority in your jurisdiction and have been assigned the same relevant topic and key number from Question 7. Provide the full citation in the official reporter to the 1984 United States Supreme Court case digested under the same topic and key number.

Questions 10a-12a: Use Shepard's print edition. If your library does not have the Shepard's in print, answer Questions 10b-17b online.
        You have decided to use the Second Circuit case from Question 3 in the memo that you are writing. You must verify that the case is still good law. You can also expand your research to other relevant cases through Shepard's. Shepardize the case in the bound main volumes.

10a.   Look at the front of the Shepard's at the "History and Treatment Abbreviations" on the inside cover of the volume. Study the abbreviations for the "History of Case." Now find the listing for the cite to your case. Is there any prior or subsequent Second Circuit case history listed? If so, give the cite.

11a.   Turn back to the abbreviations at the front of the volume. Look at the abbreviations under "Treatment of Case." Note that your case has been cited in several other Second Circuit cases. As you proceed in your research, you will need to look at these cases to determine if these cases are relevant to your issue. State the **first listed** cite of the case that distinguished your case.

12a.   Examine the case listings under the Second Circuit. Have any of the cases cited *Cunningham* for the point of law discussed in the fifth headnote? If so, provide the cite of the **first listed** entry.

Look up the case from Question 12a.

13a.   What is the name of the case?

14a.   Does the case discuss the issue of disqualification of counsel in a criminal case?

Complete Questions 10b-17b if your library does NOT have the Shepard's volumes in print. Use Shepard's online for Questions 10b-13b and Westlaw's KeyCite service for Questions 14b-17b.
Logon to http://www.lexisnexis.com/shepards/ or http://www/lexisnexis.com/lawschool.
Shepardize the case from Question 3.

10b. Examine the Shepard's summary box at the top. What does the Shepard's signal for your case indicate?

11b. How many Second Circuit **appellate** cases have cited to your case? As you proceed in your research, you will need to determine if these cases are relevant to your issue.

12b. Does your case have any citing references that give cautionary analyses? If so, what is the cite of the 1983 Second Circuit case distinguishing your case?

13b. Click on the name of the case from Question 12b. Does the case discuss disqualification of counsel?

Logon to Westlaw's KeyCite service at http://lawschool.westlaw.com. KeyCite the case from Question 3.

14b. Does KeyCite indicate any negative indirect history for your case?

15b. Negative indirect history cases from your jurisdiction can be very important to your research. How many of these are **appellate** cases from the Second Circuit?

16b. Click on the Citing References link and then Limit KeyCite Display. Limit your citing references by jurisdiction to Second Circuit Court of Appeals cases. How many cases do you get?

17b. What is the name of the 1989 Second Circuit Court of Appeals case that "examined" your case?

ASSIGNMENT SEVEN
REVIEW--FINDING, CITING AND UPDATING CASES
EXERCISE B

GOALS OF THIS ASSIGNMENT:
To review the use of digests, citators in print or online and A.L.R. to find cases.
To combine several steps of a research strategy using different types of materials.

Two days ago, Jean Tellson hired the K.J. Corey law firm for which you are working as a summer associate in Springfield, Illinois to represent her. Mrs. Tellson has been charged with possession with intent to distribute cocaine. According to the client, Mrs. Tellson was at work when the police rang the doorbell to her house she alone owns but resides with her husband Raymond. Raymond answered the door and allowed the police officers to search the residence without a search warrant. When the officers asked Raymond if they could search the backyard storage shed, Raymond produced a key and opened the shed for the officers. Subsequently, the officers found a large quantity of cocaine in a shoebox in the shed and arrested Mrs. Tellson when she arrived home from work. Attorney Knight thinks we may be able to suppress the evidence from the search and seizure since Raymond was simply a cotenant and not the owner of the house nor the shed. Knight would like you to research **federal cases** concerning the admissibility of evidence discovered in a **search and seizure** of property authorized by a **spouse** who is a **cotenant** of the residence. Please research federal case law to determine how the court may deal with this situation. Before you begin, identify the federal jurisdiction that includes Illinois and determine which courts' cases will be mandatory authority in that jurisdiction.

1.   If you are unfamiliar with a topic and looking for citations to primary authority for your jurisdiction, a good place to begin your research is in the A.L.R. Go to the A.L.R. Index and look for an A.L.R. Fed. annotation that may help you research this issue. What is the cite to the annotation?

Find the 154 A.L.R. Fed. annotation.

2.   What is the correct citation of the annotation itself? (See Rule 16.6.6 of *The Bluebook*.)

3.   In section 11, does this annotation provide you with a cite to a 1989 United States Court of Appeals Seventh Circuit case? If so, provide the full citation in correct format.

Find the case from Question 3 and read it.

4.   Given your fact situation, is this case on point?

5.   Assuming your case will take place in a federal district court in Illinois, is this case mandatory authority?

6.   Look at the headnotes of this case. Several headnotes are relevant to your issue. Which headnote discusses the wife's possession of a key as giving her apparent authority to consent to a search of a room? List its number, e.g., first, second, third, etc.

7.   What is the topic and key number of this headnote?

8.   Read the opinion corresponding to the point of law for the above headnote. According to this opinion, which provision of the United States Constitution requires a search to be reasonable?

9.   Use *West's Federal Practice Digest 4th* to find other cases that are mandatory authority in your jurisdiction and have been assigned the same relevant topic and key number from Question 7. Provide the full citation to the 1994 Seventh Circuit case arising out of Illinois that was digested under the same topic and key number.

Questions 10a-12a: Use Shepard's print edition. If your library does not have the Shepard's in print, answer Questions 10b-17b online.

You have decided to use the Seventh Circuit case from Question 3 in the memo that you are writing. You must verify that the case is still good law. You can also expand your research to other relevant cases through Shepard's. Shepardize the case in the bound main volumes.

10a. Look at the front of the Shepard's at the "History and Treatment Abbreviations" on the inside cover of the volume. Study the abbreviations for the "History of Case." Now find the listing for the cite to your case. Is there any prior or subsequent case history listed? If so, give the cite.

11a. Turn back to the abbreviations at the front of the volume. Look at the abbreviations under "Treatment of Case." Note that your case has been cited in several other Seventh Circuit cases. As you proceed in your research, you will need to look at these cases to determine if these cases are relevant to your issue. State the cite of the case that distinguished your case.

12a. Examine the case listings under the Seventh Circuit. Have any of the cases cited *Rodriguez* for the point of law discussed in the third headnote? If so, list the cite.

Look up the case from Question 12a.

13a. What is the name of the case?

14a. Does the case discuss the issue of third party authority to consent to search?

**Complete Questions 10b-17b if your library does NOT have the Shepard's volumes in print. Use Shepard's online for Questions 10b-13b and Westlaw's KeyCite service for Questions 14b-17b.
Logon to http://www.lexisnexis.com/shepards/ or http://www.lexisnexis.con/lawschool.
Shepardize the case from Question 3.**

10b.   Examine the Shepard's summary box at the top. What does the Shepard's signal for your case indicate?

11b.   How many Seventh Circuit **appellate** cases have cited to your case? As you proceed in your research, you will need to determine if these cases are relevant to your issue.

12b.   Does your case have any citing references that give positive analyses? If so, what is the name of the 2003 U.S. district court case within the Seventh Circuit that distinguished your case?

13b.   Click on the name of the case from Question 12b. Does the case deal with third party apparent authority to consent to search?

Logon to Westlaw's KeyCite service at http://lawschool.westlaw.com. KeyCite the case from Question 3.

14b.   Does KeyCite indicate any negative indirect history for your case?

15b.   Negative indirect history cases from your jurisdiction can be very important to your research. How many of these are **appellate** cases from the Seventh Circuit?

16b.   Click on the Citing References link and then Limit KeyCite Display. Limit your citing references by jurisdiction to Seventh Circuit Court of Appeals cases. How many cases do you get?

17b.   What is the name of the 2000 Seventh Circuit Court of Appeals case that distinguished your case?

ASSIGNMENT SEVEN
REVIEW--FINDING, CITING AND UPDATING CASES
EXERCISE C

GOALS OF THIS ASSIGNMENT:
To review the use of digests, citators in print or online and A.L.R. to find cases.
To combine several steps of a research strategy using different types of materials.

The law firm for which you are working as a summer associate in Chicago, Illinois is all abuzz about the happenings in court yesterday involving one of the firm's attorneys Robert Felix. Attorney Felix has been representing a defendant in a federal criminal case involving embezzlement. Throughout the trial, the judge has been very agitated with Felix and is constantly criticizing the attorney's tactics in front of the jury. Yesterday seemed to be the last straw for the judge. During Felix's closing remarks, he made reference to a witness's statement that the judge had rule inadmissible during the trial and had instructed the jury to disregard. The judge said, "What diploma mill gave you your law degree? Every attorney knows that mentioning that statement is inappropriate. You and your guilty client must truly be desperate." Attorney Felix thinks he may be able to move for a new trial due to the judge's critical remarks towards him in the presence of the jury. Please research federal case law to determine when the court finds **justification** or **excusal** of remarks made by federal trial **judges** as opposed to when the court will find the actions of the judge requires a **new trial**. Before you begin, identify the federal jurisdiction that includes Illinois and determine which courts' cases will be mandatory authority in that jurisdiction.

1.   If you are unfamiliar with a topic and looking for citations to primary authority for your jurisdiction, a good place to begin your research is in the A.L.R. Go to the A.L.R. Index and look for an A.L.R. Fed. annotation that may help you research this issue. What is the cite to the annotation?

Find the 170 A.L.R. Fed. annotation.

2.   What is the correct citation of the annotation itself? (See Rule 16.6.6 of *The Bluebook*.)

3.   In section 4[b], does this annotation provide you with a cite to a 1977 United States Court of Appeals Seventh Circuit case? If so, provide the full citation in correct format.

Find the case from Question 3 and read it.

4.   Given your fact situation, is this case on point?

5.   Assuming your case will take place in a federal district court in Illinois, is this case mandatory authority?

6.   Look at the headnotes of this case. One headnote is relevant to your issue. Which headnote discusses the denial of a fair trial by trial judge rebuking defense counsel before the jury? List its number, e.g., first, second, third, etc.

7.   What is the topic and key number of this headnote?

8.   Read the opinion corresponding to the point of law for the above headnote. According to this opinion, the court notes that the defense counsel engaged in conduct for which he deserved reprimand and censure. Where should such reprimand and censure have taken place?

9.   Use *West's Federal Practice Digest 4th* to find other cases that are mandatory authority in your jurisdiction and have been assigned the same relevant topic and key number from Question 7. Provide the full citation to the 1995 United States Court of Appeals Seventh Circuit case digested under the same topic and key number.

Questions 10a-12a: Use Shepard's print edition. If your library does not have the Shepard's in print, answer Questions 10b-17b online.
    You have decided to use the Seventh Circuit case from Question 3 in the memo that you are writing. You must verify that the case is still good law. You can also expand your research to other relevant cases through Shepard's. Shepardize the case in the bound main volumes.

10a. Look at the front of the Shepard's at the "History and Treatment Abbreviations" on the inside cover of the volume. Study the abbreviations for the "History of Case." Now find the listing for the cite to your case. Is there any prior or subsequent case history listed?

11a. Turn back to the abbreviations at the front of the volume. Look at the abbreviations under "Treatment of Case." Note that your case has been cited in several other Seventh Circuit cases. As you proceed in your research, you will need to look at these cases to determine if these cases are relevant to your issue. State the **first listed** cite of the case that distinguished your case.

12a. Examine the case listings under the Seventh Circuit. Have any of the cases cited *Spears* for the point of law discussed in the second headnote? If so, give the **second listed** cite.

Look up the case from Question 12a.

13a. What is the name of the case?

14a. Does the case discuss the issue of judicial remarks or conduct as to defense counsel in presence of the jury?

Complete Questions 10b-17b if your library does NOT have the Shepard's volumes in print. Use Shepard's online for Questions 10b-13b and Westlaw's KeyCite service for Questions 14b-17b.
Logon to http://www.lexisnexis.com/shepards/ or http://www.lexisnexis.com/lawschool/.
Shepardize the case from Question 3.

10b.   Examine the Shepard's summary box at the top. What does the Shepard's signal for your case indicate?

11b.   How many Seventh Circuit **appellate** cases have cited to your case? As you proceed in your research, you will need to determine if these cases are relevant to your issue.

12b.   Does your case have any citing references that give cautionary analyses? If so, what is the name of the 1992 Seventh Circuit case that distinguished your case?

13b.   Click on the name of the case from Question 12b. Does the case deal with allegations that judicial behavior towards attorney denied defendant a fair trial?

Logon to Westlaw's KeyCite service at http://lawschool.westlaw.com. KeyCite the case from Question 3.

14b.   Does KeyCite indicate any negative indirect history for your case?

15b.   Negative indirect history cases from your jurisdiction can be very important to your research. How many of these are **appellate** cases from the Seventh Circuit?

16b.   Click on the Citing References link and then Limit KeyCite Display. Limit your citing references by jurisdiction to Seventh Circuit Court of Appeals cases. How many cases do you get?

17b.   What is the name of the 1988 Seventh Circuit Court of Appeals case that "cited" your case?

GOALS OF THIS ASSIGNMENT:
To review the use of digests, citators in print or online and A.L.R. to find cases.
To combine several steps of a research strategy using different types of materials.

One of the partners for the law firm for which you are working as a summer associate in Buffalo, New York has sought you out to conduct some research for him. Attorney James Scott is representing a criminal defendant in a federal firearms case that is currently in its third week of trial. Attorney Scott received an anonymous tip today that someone has been communicating with at least one of the jurors. The tipster indicated that juror #4 had received two non-threatening notes. The first note said, "You have beautiful green eyes." The second note said, "Are you married?" In addition, juror #4 has received several phone calls in which the anonymous caller hangs up when she answers the phone. Attorney Scott believes unauthorized communications to a **jury** and, in particular, the **stranger's communications** with this juror, are **prejudicial** to the **jury trial**. Please research federal case law to determine how the court may deal with this situation. Before you begin, identify the federal jurisdiction that includes New York and determine which courts' cases will be mandatory authority in that jurisdiction.

1. If you are unfamiliar with a topic and looking for citations to primary authority for your jurisdiction, a good place to begin your research is in the A.L.R. Go to the A.L.R. Index and look for an A.L.R. Fed. annotation that may help you research this issue. What is the cite to the annotation?

Find the 131 A.L.R. Fed. annotation.

2. What is the correct citation of the annotation itself? (See Rule 16.6.6 of *The Bluebook*.)

3.   In section 40, does this annotation provide you with a cite to a 1964 United States Court of Appeals Second Circuit case? If so, provide the full citation in correct format.

Find the case from Question 3 and read it.

4.   Given your fact situation, is this case on point?

5.   Assuming your case will take place in a federal district court in New York, is this case mandatory authority?

6.   Look at the headnotes of this case. Several headnotes are relevant to your issue. Which headnote discusses that the court is not bound to order a new trial unless outside contact with juror conclusively shows prejudice? List its number, e.g., first, second, third, etc.

7.   What is the topic and key number of this headnote?

8.   Read the opinion corresponding to the point of law for the above headnote. According to this opinion, did the defense request a hearing to investigate the potential impact of the phone calls on the juror or other jurors?

9.   Use *West's Federal Practice Digest 4th* to find other cases that are mandatory authority in your jurisdiction and have been assigned the same relevant topic and key number from Question 7. Provide the full citation to the **first listed** 1989 United States Court of Appeals Second Circuit case digested under the same topic and key number.

Questions 10a-12a: Use Shepard's print edition. If your library does not have the Shepard's in print, answer Questions 10b-17b online.
        You have decided to use the Second Circuit case from Question 3 in the memo that you are writing. You must verify that the case is still good law. You can also expand your research to other relevant cases through Shepard's. Shepardize the case in the bound main volumes.

10a. Look at the front of the Shepard's at the "History and Treatment Abbreviations" on the inside cover of the volume. Study the abbreviations for the "History of Case." Now find the listing for the cite to your case. Is there any prior or subsequent case history listed? If so, provide the cite to the **first listed** entry.

11a. Turn back to the abbreviations at the front of the volume. Look at the abbreviations under "Treatment of Case." Note that your case has been cited in several other Second Circuit cases. As you proceed in your research, you will need to look at these cases to determine if these cases are relevant to your issue. State the **first listed** cite of the case that distinguished your case.

12a. Examine the case listings under the Second Circuit. Have any of the cases cited *Gersh* for the point of law discussed in the fifth headnote? If so, give the **second listed** cite.

Look up the case from Question 12a.

13a. What is the name of the case?

14a. Does the case discuss the issue of third party communications with jurors?

Complete Questions 10b-17b if your library does NOT have the Shepard's volumes in print. Use Shepard's online for Questions 10b-13b and Westlaw's KeyCite service for Questions 14b-17b.
Logon to http://www.lexisnexis.com/shepards/ or http://www.lexisnexis.com/lawschool/.
Shepardize the case from Question 3.

10b. Examine the Shepard's summary box at the top. What does the Shepard's signal for your case indicate?

11b. How many Second Circuit **appellate** cases have cited to your case? As you proceed in your research, you will need to determine if these cases are relevant to your issue.

12b. Does your case have any citing references that give cautionary analyses? If so, what is the name of the 1968 Second Circuit case that distinguished your case?

13b. Click on the name of the case from Question 12b. Does the case deal with third party communications with jurors?

Logon to Westlaw's KeyCite service at http://lawschool.westlaw.com. KeyCite the case from Question 3.

14b. Does KeyCite indicate any negative indirect history for your case?

15b. Negative indirect history cases from your jurisdiction can be very important to your research. How many of these are **appellate** cases from the Second Circuit?

16b. Click on the Citing References link and then Limit KeyCite Display. Limit your citing references by jurisdiction to Second Circuit Court of Appeals cases. How many cases do you get?

17b. What is the name of the **first listed** 1975 Second Circuit Court of Appeals case that "cited" your case?

ASSIGNMENT EIGHT
FINDING AND CITING STATUTES
EXERCISE A

GOALS OF THIS ASSIGNMENT:
To acquaint you with finding federal and state statutes in your library.
To familiarize you with the rules for citing statutes in *The Bluebook: A Uniform System of Citation*, 18th ed.

CITATION RULES: You will need to read and apply Rule 12 (including its subsections) and review table T.1 in *The Bluebook*. In this assignment we give you either a citation or a subject area and you must find federal and state statutes. Once you have found the statutes, you must cite them correctly.

The first three questions require you to find and cite a statute in the official federal code, the *United States Code* (U.S.C.). The citation includes the title number, the code abbreviation, the section number(s), the date of the code appearing on the spine, and the supplement date (if the act appears in the supplement). Include the name of the act or the act's popular name and the original uncodified section of the act if such information would aid in identification. **Example: 23 U.S.C. § 126 (2000).**

1. For statutes currently in force, which code should you cite?

2. What is the date of the current edition of the U.S.C.?

3. Find and cite the *United States Code*, title 45, sections 231 to 231b. Use the current edition (not the supplements). Do not include the name of the act.

The next question requires you to find and cite a statute in one of the unofficial federal codes, *United States Code Annotated* (U.S.C.A.). You may cite unofficial codes (U.S.C.A. and U.S.C.S.) when the statute is too recent to appear in the U.S.C. Include the information you used for the U.S.C., in addition to the name of the publisher. You must also include the precise location in either U.S.C.A. or U.S.C.S. where the statute appears. Cite to either the main volume, the pocket part, or both. Since no date appears on the spine of the main volume, the year cited is the copyright date.
Example: 10 U.S.C.A. § 9344 (West 1998 & Supp. 2004).

4.   Find and cite § 231 of Title 45 of U.S.C.A. correctly.

Next you must find and cite a federal session law using *United States Statutes at Large*. According to Rule 12.4 of *The Bluebook*, when citing session laws, always give the name of the statute, the public law number, volume and page number of the Statutes at Large (Stat.), and the year of passage if not revealed in its name. **Example: Home Energy Assistance Act of 1980, Pub. L. No. 96-223, 94 Stat. 288.**

5.   Find and cite 113 Stat. 41.

For the next two questions, find and cite a state statute in a code. We require that you use the index to find the correct act. When citing a state code, include the name of the code; the chapter, title, or other subdivision; possibly the name of the publisher; and the year of the code. You must use table T.1 to determine proper citation format for individual jurisdictions. **Example: Miss. Code Ann. § 75-5-109 (2004).**

6.   Use the index to the *Florida Statutes Annotated* and find a statute that names the dolphin as the state saltwater mammal.

For some states, most notably California, Texas and New York, include the subject on the spine as part of the name of the code. **Example: Tex. Educ. Code Ann. § 11.058 (Vernon 2000).**

7.   Use the index to the *Annotated California Code* and find a statute that defines surf boarding as a water contact sport.

Statutes are online on WESTLAW and LEXIS and free Internet sites. You can search for statutes by subject area or citation. On WESTLAW, you can retrieve statutes if you have the citation with the FIND command. On LEXIS, use GET A DOCUMENT to locate statutes.

ASSIGNMENT EIGHT
FINDING AND CITING STATUTES
EXERCISE B

GOALS OF THIS ASSIGNMENT:
To acquaint you with finding federal and state statutes in your library.
To familiarize you with the rules for citing statutes in *The Bluebook: A Uniform System of Citation*, 18th ed.

CITATION RULES: You will need to read and apply Rule 12 (including its subsections) and review table T.1 in *The Bluebook*. In this assignment we give you either a citation or a subject area and you must find federal and state statutes. Once you have found the statutes, you must cite them correctly.

The first three questions require you to find and cite a statute in the official federal code, the *United States Code* (U.S.C.). The citation includes the title number, the code abbreviation, the section number(s), the date of the code appearing on the spine, and the supplement date (if the act appears in the supplement). Include the name of the act or the act's popular name and the original uncodified section of the act if such information would aid in identification. **Example: 23 U.S.C. § 126 (2000).**

1.   For statutes currently in force, which code should you cite?

2.   What is the date of the current edition of the U.S.C.?

3.   Find and cite the *United States Code*, title 29, sections 621 to 634. Use the current edition (not the supplements). Do not include the name of the act.

The next question requires you to find and cite a statute in one of the unofficial federal codes, *United States Code Annotated* (U.S.C.A.). You may cite unofficial codes (U.S.C.A. and U.S.C.S.) when the statute is too recent to appear in the U.S.C. Include the information you used for the U.S.C., in addition to the name of the publisher. You must also include the precise location in either U.S.C.A. or U.S.C.S. where the statute appears. Cite to either the main volume, the pocket part, or both. Since no date appears on the spine of the main volume, the year cited is the copyright date. **Example: 10 U.S.C.A. § 9344 (West 1998 & Supp. 2004).**

4.   Find and cite § 623 of Title 29 of U.S.C.A. correctly.

Next you must find and cite a federal session law using *United States Statutes at Large*. According to Rule 12.4 of *The Bluebook*, when citing session laws, always give the name of the statute, the public law number, volume and page number of the Statutes at Large (Stat.), and the year of passage if not revealed in its name. **Example: Home Energy Assistance Act of 1980, Pub. L. No. 96-223, 94 Stat. 288.**

5.   Find and cite 112 Stat. 2919.

For the next two questions, find and cite a state statute in a code. We require that you use the index to locate the correct act. When citing a state code, include the name of the code; the chapter, title, or other subdivision; possibly the name of the publisher; and the year of the code. You must use table T.1 to determine proper citation formats for individual jurisdictions. **Example: Miss. Code Ann. § 75-5-109 (2004).**

6.   Use the index to the *Code of Alabama* and find a statute prohibiting selling ducks.

For some states, most notably California, Texas and New York, include the subject on the spine as part of the name of the code. **Example: Tex. Educ. Code Ann. § 11.058 (Vernon 2000).**

7.   Use the index to the *Texas Codes Annotated* and locate a statute restricting a person from operating hay loaders under certain circumstances.

Statutes are online on WESTLAW and LEXIS and free Internet sites. You can search for statutes by subject area or citation. On WESTLAW, you can retrieve statutes if you have the citation with the FIND command. On LEXIS, use GET A DOCUMENT to locate statutes.

ASSIGNMENT EIGHT
FINDING AND CITING STATUTES
EXERCISE C

GOALS OF THIS ASSIGNMENT:
To acquaint you with finding federal and state statutes in your library.
To familiarize you with the rules for citing statutes in *The Bluebook: A Uniform System of Citation*, 18th ed.

CITATION RULES: You will need to read and apply Rule 12 (including its subsections) and review table T.1 in *The Bluebook*. In this assignment we give you either a citation or a subject area and you must find federal and state statutes. Once you have found the statutes, you must cite them correctly.

The three first questions require you to find and cite a statute in the official federal code, the *United States Code* (U.S.C.). The citation includes the title number, the code abbreviation, the section number(s), the date of the code appearing on the spine, and the supplement date (if the act appears in the supplement). Include the name of the act or the act's popular name and the original uncodified section of the act if such information would aid in identification. **Example: 23 U.S.C. § 126 (2000).**

1. For statutes currently in force, which code should you cite?

2. What is the date of the current edition of the U.S.C.?

3. Find and cite the *United States Code*, title 22, sections 1360 to 1385. Use the current edition (not the supplements). Do not include the name of the act.

The next question requires you to find and cite a statute in one of the unofficial federal codes, *United States Code Annotated* (U.S.C.A.). You may cite unofficial codes (U.S.C.A. and U.S.C.S.) when the statute is too recent to appear in the U.S.C. Include the information you used for the U.S.C., in addition to the name of the publisher. You must also include the precise location in either U.S.C.A. or U.S.C.S. where the statute appears. Cite to either the main volume, the pocket part, or both. Since no date appears on the spine of the main volume, the year cited is the copyright date. **Example: 10 U.S.C.A. § 9344 (West 1998 & Supp. 2004).**

4.   Find and cite § 420 of Title 24 of U.S.C.A. correctly.

Next you must find and cite a federal session law using *United States Statutes at Large*. According to Rule 12.4 of *The Bluebook*, when citing session laws, always give the name of the statute, the public law number, volume and page number of the Statutes at Large (Stat.), and the year of passage if not revealed in its name. **Example: Home Energy Assistance Act of 1980, Pub. L. No. 96-223, 94 Stat. 288.**

5.   Find and cite 114 Stat. 251.

For the next two questions, find and cite a state statute in a code. We require that you use the index to locate the correct act. When citing a state code, include the name of the code; the chapter, title, or other subdivision; possibly the name of the publisher; and the year of the code. You must use table T.1 to determine proper citation format for individual jurisdictions. **Example: Miss. Code Ann. § 75-5-109 (2004).**

6.   Use the index to the *Code of Laws of South Carolina* and find a statute indicating whether toy pistols are considered fireworks.

For some states, most notably California, Texas and New York, include the subject on the spine as part of the name of the code. **Example: Tex. Educ. Code Ann. § 11.058 (West 2000).**

7.   Use the index to the *Annotated California Code* and find a statute on what is considered a wine grape product.

Statutes are online on WESTLAW and LEXIS and free Internet sites. You can search for statutes by subject area or citation. On WESTLAW, you can retrieve statutes if you have the citation with the FIND command. On LEXIS, use GET A DOCUMENT to locate statutes.

ASSIGNMENT EIGHT
FINDING AND CITING STATUTES
EXERCISE D

GOALS OF THIS ASSIGNMENT:
To acquaint you with finding federal and state statutes in your library.
To familiarize you with the rules for citing statutes in *The Bluebook: A Uniform System of Citation*, 18th ed.

CITATION RULES: You will need to read and apply Rule 12 (including its subsections) and review table T.1 in *The Bluebook*. In this assignment we give you either a citation or a subject area and you must find federal and state statutes. Once you have found the statutes, you must cite them correctly.

The first three questions require you to find and cite a statute in the official federal code, the *United States Code* (U.S.C.). The citation includes the title number, the code abbreviation, the section number(s), the date of the code appearing on the spine, and the supplement date (if the act appears in the supplement). Include the name of the act or the act's popular name and the original uncodified section of the act if such information would aid in identification. **Example: 23 U.S.C. § 126 (2000).**

1.   For statutes currently in force, which code should you cite?

2.   What is the date of the current edition of the U.S.C.?

3.   Find and cite the *United States Code*, title 10, sections 2241 to 2259. Use the current edition (not the supplements). Do not include the name of the act.

The next question requires you to find and cite a statute in one of the unofficial federal codes, *United States Code Annotated* (U.S.C.A.). You may cite unofficial codes (U.S.C.A. and U.S.C.S.) when the statute is too recent to appear in the U.S.C. Include the information you used for the U.S.C., in addition to the name of the publisher. You must also include the precise location in either U.S.C.A. or U.S.C.S. where the statute appears. Cite to either the main volume, the pocket part, or both. Since no date appears on the spine of the main volume, the year cited is the copyright date. **Example: 10 U.S.C.A. § 9344 (West 1998 & Supp. 2004).**

4.   Find and cite § 2218 of Title 10 of U.S.C.A. correctly.

Next you must find and cite a federal session law using *United States Statutes at Large*. According to *The Bluebook*, when citing session laws, always give the name of the statute, the public law number, volume and page number of the Statutes at Large (Stat.), and the year of passage if not revealed in its name. **Example: Home Energy Assistance Act of 1980, Pub. L. No. 96-223, 94 Stat. 288.**

5.   Find and cite 107 Stat. 6.

For the next two questions, find and cite a state statute in a code. We require that you use the index to locate the correct act. When citing a state code, include the name of the code; the chapter, title, or other subdivision; possibly the name of the publisher; and the year of the code. You must use table T.1 to determine proper citation formats for individual jurisdictions. **Example: Miss. Code Ann. § 75-5-109 (2004).**

6.   Use the index to the *Michigan Compiled Laws Annotated* and find a statute requiring a license for a person to operate a snow motor.

For some states, most notably California, Texas and New York, include the subject on the spine as part of the name of the code. **Example: Tex. Educ. Code Ann. § 11.058 (West 2000).**

7.   Use the index to the *McKinney's Consolidated Laws of New York Annotated* or *Consolidated Laws Service* and find a statute dealing with railroad companies transporting the United States mail.

Statutes are online on WESTLAW and LEXIS and free Internet sites. On WESTLAW, you can retrieve statutes if you have the citation with the FIND command. On LEXIS, use GET A DOCUMENT to locate statutes.

ASSIGNMENT NINE
FEDERAL CODES AND SESSION LAWS
EXERCISE A

GOALS OF THIS ASSIGNMENT:
To reveal the similarities and differences between the two annotated codes.
To introduce you to federal session laws.
To introduce you to the legislative history materials available in *U.S. Code Congressional & Administrative News.*

1. Use the index in U.S.C.A. to find the title and section of the code to answer the following question. What must be included in a Foreign Service Grievance Board decision? Answer the question and provide the citation to the code. Note: In *The Bluebook*, use Rule 12 and table T.1

    In your research you will seldom, if ever, use the "official" U.S. Code, because it is not current and does not contain annotations. Therefore to answer Questions 2-7, use the two annotated codes, U.S.C.A. and U.S.C.S., of the code section you found in Question 1. **Be sure to check the pocket parts and the supplementary pamphlets for possible updates!**

2. Look up the text of the statute from Question 1. Next, look at the information in parentheses at the end of the section. State the date, public law number, and *U.S. Statutes at Large* citation for the 1980 act passed during the 96th Congress.

3. a. Which code (U.S.C.A. or U.S.C.S.) refers you to the specific Code of Federal Regulations provision on burden of proof?
    b. What is the citation (title and part)?
        a.
        b.

4. a. Which codes refer you to Federal Procedure, L. Ed.?
    b. List the sections of Federal Procedure, L. Ed. provided.
        a.
        b.

5. a. Which code refers you to topic and key numbers in the American Digest System?
    b. List the **first listed** topic and key number.
        a.
        b.

6. a. Which codes refer you to court decisions?
    b. State the **name** of the 1987 federal district court decision.
        a.
        b.

7. a. Which code refers you to electronic research?
    b. What system does the code refer you to?
        a.
        b.

Reshelve the unofficial codes.

Remember that a code is a subject arrangement of current, general laws. Note how helpful the unofficial codes can be since they refer you to cases, encyclopedia articles, law review articles, digests, and secondary materials.

Now, assume that you want to look at the text of 112 Stat. 1253.

To find the text of a law or amendment as Congress passed it, use the *U.S. Statutes at Large* for Questions 8-10.

8.   Find 112 Stat. 1253. Go to the beginning of the Public Law at 112 Stat. 1253. What is the Public Law number?

9.   What is the bill number for the act?

10.   Examine the last page of the act. When was this act approved?

Now assume that you wish to see some legislative history for this act. Legislative history refers to committee reports, legislative debates and hearings generated during the consideration of bills. Courts often consider legislative history when interpreting a statute because legislative history can show legislative intent.

***U.S. Code Congressional & Administrative News* (U.S.C.C.A.N.) is an accessible source of legislative history and the text of public laws (Questions 11-12).**

11.   The text of the public law you already examined in 112 Stat. 1253 is also reprinted in U.S.C.C.A.N. in 1998, vol. 2. Look it up. Where can you locate the **Legislative History** for the act?

12.   Look up the legislative history (it is in vol. 4). Which House Report is reprinted?

You have now found the current text of a statute, examined the text as Congress passed it into law and looked at some of its legislative history.

ASSIGNMENT NINE
FEDERAL CODES AND SESSION LAWS
EXERCISE B

GOALS OF THIS ASSIGNMENT:
To reveal the similarities and differences between the two annotated codes.
To introduce you to federal session laws.
To introduce you to the legislative history materials available in *U.S. Code Congressional & Administrative News*.

1.   Use the index in U.S.C.A. to find the title and section of the code to answer the following question. If an employer violates the Employee Polygraph Protection Act, how much may the employer be fined? Note: In *The Bluebook*, use Rule 12 and table T.1.

In your research you will seldom, if ever, use the "official" U.S. Code, because it is not current and does not contain annotations. Therefore to answer Questions 2-7, use the two annotated codes, U.S.C.A. and U.S.C.S., of the code section you found in Question 1. **Be sure to check the pocket parts and the supplementary pamphlets for possible updates!**

2.   Look up the text of the statute from Question 1. Next, look at the information in parentheses at the end of the section. State the date, public law number, and *U.S. Statutes at Large* citation reference for the act.

3.   a.   Which codes (U.S.C.A. and/or U.S.C.S.) cite to the Code of Federal Regulations? What is the specific citation on enforcement?
         b.   State the C.F.R. citation (title and section).
                        a.
                        b.

4. a.   Which code refers you to the 1992 *Canto v. Sheraton-Carlton Hotel* case that appeared in both BNA and CCH looseleaf services?
    b.   What is the CCH citation?
                  a.
                  b.

5. a.   Which code refers you to electronic research?
    b.   What system does the code refer you to?
                  a.
                  b.

6. a.   Which codes cites to Am. Jur. 2d?
    b.   What are the volume numbers of Am. Jur. 2d?
                  a.
                  b.

7. a.   Which code provides a cross reference to a law review article by Martin H. Malin and Robert F. Ladenson?
    b.   What is the citation to the law review?
                  a.
                  b.

Reshelve the unofficial codes.

Remember that a code is a subject arrangement of current, general laws. Note how helpful the unofficial codes (U.S.C.A. and U.S.C.S.) can be since they refer you to cases, encyclopedia articles, law review articles, digests, and secondary materials.

Now assume that you want to look at the text of 114 Stat. 2423.

To find the text of a law or amendment as Congress passed it, use the *U.S. Statutes at Large* for Questions 8-10.

8.   Find 114 Stat. 2423. Go to the beginning of the Public Law at 114 Stat. 2423. What is the Public Law number?

9.   What is the bill number for the act?

10.   Examine the last page of the act. When was this act approved?

Now assume that you wish to see some legislative history for this act. Legislative history refers to committee reports, legislative debates and hearings generated during the consideration of bills. Courts often consider legislative history when interpreting a statute because legislative history can show legislative intent.

***U.S. Code Congressional & Administrative News* (U.S.C.C.A.N.) is an accessible source of legislative history and the text of public laws (Questions 11-12).**

11.   The text of the act you already examined in 114 Stat. 2423 is also reprinted in U.S.C.C.A.N. in 2000, vol. 3.   Look it up. Where can you locate the **Legislative History** for the act?

12.   Look up the legislative history (it is in vol. 5). Which House Report is reprinted?

You have now found the current text of a statute, examined the text as Congress passed it into law, and looked at some of its legislative history.

ASSIGNMENT NINE
FEDERAL CODES AND SESSION LAWS
EXERCISE C

GOALS OF THIS ASSIGNMENT:
To reveal the similarities and differences between the two annotated codes.
To introduce you to federal session laws.
To introduce you to the legislative history materials available in *U.S. Code Congressional & Administrative News*.

1. Use the index in U.S.C.A. to find the title and section of the code to answer the following question: Who is responsible for the federal enforcement of drinking water supply? Note: In *The Bluebook*, use Rule12 and table T.1.

    In your research you will seldom, if ever, use the "official" U.S. Code, because it is not current and does not contain annotations. Therefore to answer Questions 2-7, use the two annotated codes, U.S.C.A. and U.S.C.S., of the code section you found in Question 1. **Be sure to check the pocket parts and the supplementary pamphlets for possible updates!**

2. Look up the text of the statute from Question 1. Next, look at the information in parentheses at the end of the section. State the date, public law number, and *U.S. Statutes at Large* citation for the 2002 amendment.

3. a. Which code (U.S.C.A. or U.S.C.S.) refers you to relevant West topic and key numbers in the American Digest System?
    b. List the **first listed** topic and key numbers.
                a.
                b.

4.   a.   Which code refers you to the Code of Federal Regulations for the OMB approvals under the Paperwork Reduction Act?

      b.   List the citation (title and part).

              a.

              b.

5.   a.   Which code refers you to law review articles?

      b.   Who is the **author** of the 1989 article that appeared in the Naval Law Review (Nav. L. Rev.)?

              a.

              b.

6.   a.   Which code refers you to C.J.S.?

      b.   What are the relevant sections under the topic *States*?

              a.

              b.

7.   a.   Which code cites to the Environmental Reporter Cases?

      b.   State the **name** of the 1983 case in the reporter.

              a.

              b.

Reshelve the unofficial codes.

Remember that a code is a subject arrangement of current, general laws. Note how helpful the unofficial codes (U.S.C.A. and U.S.C.S.) can be since they refer you to cases, encyclopedia articles, law reviews, and digests.

Now assume that you want to look at the text of 116 Stat. 3078.

To find the text of a law or amendment as Congress passed it, use the *U.S. Statutes at Large* for Questions 8-10.

8. Find 116 Stat. 3078. Go to the beginning of the Public Law at 116 Stat. 3078. What is the Public Law number?

9. What is the bill number for the act?

10. Examine the last page of the act. When was this act approved?

Now assume that you wish to see some legislative history for this act. Legislative history refers to committee reports, legislative debates and hearings generated during the consideration of bills. Courts often consider legislative history when interpreting a statute because legislative history can show legislative intent.

U.S. *Code Congressional & Administrative News* (U.S.C.C.A.N.) is an accessible source of legislative history and the text of public laws (Questions 11-12).

11. The text of the public law you already examined in 116 Stat. 3078 is also reprinted in U.S.C.C.A.N. in 2002, vol. 3. Look it up. Where can you locate the **Legislative History** for the act?

12. Look up the legislative history (it is in vol. 4). Which House Report is reprinted?

You have now found the current text of a statute, examined the text as Congress passed it into law and looked at some of its legislative history.

ASSIGNMENT NINE
FEDERAL CODES AND SESSION LAWS
EXERCISE D

GOALS OF THIS ASSIGNMENT:
To reveal the similarities and differences between the two annotated codes.
To introduce you to federal session laws.
To introduce you to the legislative history materials available in *U.S. Code*
Congressional & Administrative News.

1. Use the index in U.S.C.A. to find the title and section of the code to answer the following question. When there is a vacancy in the office of U.S. Attorney General, who is in charge of that office? Answer the question and provide the citation to the code. Note: In *The Bluebook*, use Rule 12 and table T.1.

    In your research you will seldom, if ever, use the "official" U.S. Code, because it is not current and does not contain annotations. Therefore to answer Questions 2-7, use the two annotated codes, U.S.C.A. and U.S.C.S., of the code section you found in Question 1. **Be sure to check the pocket parts and the supplementary pamphlets for possible updates!**

2. Look up the text of the statute from Question 1. Next, look at the information in parentheses at the end of the section. State the date, public law number, and *U.S. Statutes at Large* citation for the 1966 act.

3. a. Which code (U.S.C.A. or U.S.C.S.) refers you to an A.L.R. annotation?
    b. List the citation to the A.L.R.
        a.
        b.

4. a. Which code refers you to a topic and key numbers in the American Digest System?

    b.   List the topic and key number.

    a.

    b.

5. a. Which code provides references to C.J.S.?

    b. State the C.J.S. citation.

    a.

    b.

6. a. Which codes contain annotations of decisions?

    b. State the name of the First Circuit Court of Appeals decision.

    a.

    b.

7. a. Which code refers you to electronic research?

    b. What system does the code refer you to?

    a.

    b.

Reshelve the unofficial codes.

Remember that a code is a subject arrangement of current, general laws. Note how helpful the unofficial codes (U.S.C.A. and U.S.C.S.) can be since they refer you to cases, encyclopedia articles, law review articles, digests, and secondary materials.

Now assume that you want to look at the text of 112 Stat. 2702.

To find the text of a law or amendment as Congress passed it, you can use
U.S. Statutes at Large **for Questions 8-10.**

8. Find 112 Stat. 2702. Go back to the beginning of the Public Law at 112 Stat. 2702. What is the Public Law number?

9. What is the bill number for the act?

10. Examine the last page of the act. On what date was this act approved?

Now assume that you wish to see some legislative history for this act. Legislative history refers to committee reports, legislative debates and hearings generated during the consideration of bills. Courts often consider legislative history when interpreting a statute because legislative history can show legislative intent.

U.S. Code Congressional & Administrative News **(U.S.C.C.A.N.) is an accessible source of legislative history and the text of public laws (Questions 11-12).**

11. The text of the public laws that you already examined in 112 Stat. 2702 are also reprinted in U.S.C.C.A.N. in1998 vol. 3. Look it up. Where can you locate the **Legislative History** for the act?

12. Look up the legislative history (it is in vol. 5). Which House Conference Report is reprinted?

You have now found the current text of a statute, examined the text as it was passed into law and looked at some of its legislative history.

ASSIGNMENT TEN
FEDERAL LEGISLATIVE HISTORY INDEXES AND WEBSITES
EXERCISE A

GOALS OF THIS ASSIGNMENT:
To acquaint you with the *CIS/Index* for accessing legislative documents.
Introduce you to the THOMAS website for accessing legislative documents.

Questions 1-11 require you to use the *CIS/Index* (CIS). *CIS/Index* is also on the web known as the LexisNexis CIS Index. Your school may subscribe to this website, **http://lexis-nexis.com/congcomp**. Refer to Rule 13 in *The Bluebook: A Uniform System of Citation*, 18th ed.

CIS gives you legislative history information and abstracts of the four types of Congressional publications: reports, documents, hearings and committee prints. **Note: H.R. is the abbreviation for the House of Representatives; S. is the abbreviation for the Senate.**

1. Assume you are seeking information on the legislative history of the act, Pub. L. No. 107-106, enacted in 2001. Start with the CIS 2001 Legislative Histories volume. Find the entry for Pub. L. No. 107-106. What is the title of the act? Note: If you are using the CIS website, click on the CIS Index, then click on Legislative Histories by number.

2. What is the June 30, 1992 Senate Report on the bill? Cite it according to Rule 13.4 of *The Bluebook*.

3. What is the CIS abstract number for the report from Question 2?

4. Next, examine the CIS abstract of the September 21, 1989 House hearings summarized in CIS90:H421-2. On what pages in the hearing can you find Rep. John Lewis' testimony?

5. To obtain the full texts of the bills, reports or hearings in your library, you might have to know the Superintendent of Documents (SuDocs) number. This number begins with a "Y" and contains a colon. What is the SuDoc number of the hearing from Question 4?

Now, you will search the THOMAS website using the same public law as Question 1. THOMAS accesses legislative information on the Internet without a fee. Go to http://thomas.loc.gov. Take a few minutes to familiarize yourself with the site.

6. Locate the **National Museum of African American History and Culture Plan for Action Presidential Commission Act of 2001**, Pub. L. No. 107-106 by first clicking on Public Laws, then 107th Congress. Next, locate the correct public law. What is the bill number that passed into law? Hint: The abbreviation "H.R." proceeds the bill number if it originated in the House of Representatives or an "S." if it originated in the Senate.

   Instruction: Click on the bill number link and then on the following page, click on "ALL Congressional Actions."

7. Who was the main sponsor of the bill?

8. To which House committees were the bill referred to on 12/11/2001?

9. When was it passed by without amendment by unanimous consent as it appeared in the *Congressional Record.*

10. Is the full text of the relevant passages in the *Congressional Record* available?

11. When did the President sign the bill?

ASSIGNMENT TEN
FEDERAL LEGISLATIVE HISTORY INDEXES AND WEBSITES
EXERCISE B

GOALS OF THIS ASSIGNMENT:
To acquaint you with the *CIS/Index* for accessing legislative documents.
Introduce you to the THOMAS website for accessing legislative documents.

Questions 1-11 require you to use the *CIS/Index* (CIS). *CIS/Index* is also on the web known as the LexisNexis CIS Index. Your school may subscribe to this website, http://lexis-nexis.com/congcomp. Refer to Rule 13 in *The Bluebook: A Uniform System of Citation*, 18th ed.

CIS gives you legislative history information and abstracts of the four types of Congressional publications: reports, documents, hearings and committee prints. **Note: H.R. is the abbreviation for the House of Representatives; S. is the abbreviation for the Senate.**

1. Assume you are seeking information on the legislative history of the act, Pub. L. No. 106-249, enacted in 2000. Start with the CIS 2000 Legislative Histories volume. Find the entry for Pub. L. No. 106-249. What is the title of the act? Note: If you are using the CIS website, click on the CIS Index, then click on Legislative Histories by number.

2. What is the 1999 Senate Report number on S. 986? Cite it according to Rule 13.4 of *The Bluebook*.

3. What is the CIS abstract number of the report from Question 2?

4. Next, examine the CIS abstract of the July 28, 1999 Senate hearings summarized in CIS00:S311-10. On what pages in the hearing can you find Harry Reid's testimony?

5. To obtain the full texts of the bills, reports or hearings in your library, you might have to know the Superintendent of Documents (SuDocs) number. This number begins with a "Y" and contains a colon. What is the SuDoc number of the hearing from Question 4?

Now, you will search the THOMAS website using the same public law as Question 1. THOMAS accesses legislative information on the Internet without a fee. Go to http://thomas.loc.gov. Take a few minutes to familiarize yourself with the site.

6.   Locate the **Griffith Project to the Southern Nevada Water Authority**, Pub. L. No. 106-249 by first clicking on Public Laws, then 106th Congress. Next, locate the correct public law. What is the bill number that passed into law? Hint: The abbreviation "H.R." proceeds the bill number if it originated in the House of Representatives or an "S." if it originated in the Senate.

Instruction: Click on the bill number link and then on the following page, click on "ALL Congressional Actions."

7.   Who was the main sponsor of the bill?

8.   To which House committee was the bill referred on 7/10/2000?

9.   What was the House Report number reported by the Committee on Resources on 7/10/2000? Cite it according to Rule 13.4 of *The Bluebook*.

10.   Is the full text of the report available?

11.   When did the President sign the bill?

GOALS OF THIS ASSIGNMENT:
To acquaint you with the *CIS/Index* for accessing legislative documents.
Introduce you to the THOMAS website for accessing legislative documents.

> **Questions 1-11 require you to use the *CIS/Index* (CIS). *CIS/Index* is also on the web known as the LexisNexis CIS Index. Your school may subscribe to this website, http://lexis-nexis.com/congcomp. Refer to Rule 13 in *The Bluebook: A Uniform System of Citation*, 18th ed.**
>
> CIS gives you legislative history information and abstracts of the four types of Congressional publications: reports, documents, hearings and committee prints. **Note: H.R. is the abbreviation for the House of Representatives; S. is the abbreviation for the Senate.**

1. Assume you are seeking information on the legislative history of the act, Pub. L. No. 107-207, enacted in 2002. Start with the 2002 CIS Legislative Histories volume. What is the title of the act?
    Note: If you are using the CIS website, click on the CIS Index, then click on Legislative Histories by number.

2. What is the 2000 House Report number on H.R. 4292? Cite it according to Rule 13.4 of *The Bluebook*.

3. What is the CIS abstract number for the report from Question 2?

4. Next, examine the CIS abstract of the 2000 House hearings summarized in CIS01:H521-18 from July 20, 2000. On what pages in the hearing can you find Robert P. George's testimony?

5. To obtain the full texts of the bills, reports or hearings in your library, you might have to know the Superintendent of Documents (SuDocs) number. This number begins with a "Y" and contains a colon. What is the SuDoc number of the hearing from Question 4?

Now, you will search the THOMAS website using the same public law as Question 1. THOMAS accesses legislative information on the Internet without a fee. Go the http://thomas.loc.gov. Take a few minutes to familiarize yourself with the site.

6. Locate the **Born-Alive Infants Protection Act of 2002**, Pub. L. No. 107-207 by first clicking on Public Laws, then the 107th Congress. Next, locate the correct public law. What is the bill number that passed into law? Hint: The abbreviation "H.R." proceeds the bill number if it originated in the House of Representatives or an "S." if it originated in the Senate.

    Instruction: Click on the bill number link and then on the following page, click on "ALL Congressional Actions."

7. Who was the main sponsor of the bill?

8. To which House committee was the bill referred on 6/14/2001?

9. What was the House Report number reported by the House Committee on Judiciary on 8/2/01? Cite it according to Rule 13.4 of *The Bluebook*.

10. Is the report available in full text?

11. When did the President sign the bill?

ASSIGNMENT TEN
FEDERAL LEGISLATIVE HISTORY INDEXES AND WEBSITES
EXERCISE D

GOALS OF THIS ASSIGNMENT:
To acquaint you with the *CIS/Index* for accessing legislative documents.
Introduce you to the THOMAS website for accessing legislative documents.

Questions 1-11 require you to use the *CIS/Index* Annual (CIS). *CIS/Index* is also on the web known as the LexisNexis CIS Index. Your school may subscribe to this website, http://lexis-nexis.com/congcomp. Refer to Rule 13 in *The Bluebook: A Uniform System of Citation*, 18th ed.

CIS gives you legislative history information and abstracts of the four types of Congressional publications: reports, documents, hearings and committee prints. **Note: H.R. is the abbreviation for the House of Representatives; S. is the abbreviation for the Senate.**

1. Assume you are seeking information on the legislative history of an act, Pub. L. No. 108-81, enacted in 2003. Start with the CIS 2003 Legislative Histories volume. Find the entry for Pub. L. No. 108-81. What is the title of the act? Note: If you are using the CIS website, click on the CIS Index, then click on Legislative Histories by number.

2. What is the 2002 House Report number on H.R. 3784? Cite it according to Rule 13.4 of *The Bluebook*.

3. What is the CIS abstract number of the report from Question 2?

4. Next, examine the CIS abstract of the April 10, 2002 hearings summarized in CIS02:S431-24. On what pages in the hearing can you find Robert S. Martin's testimony?

5. To obtain the full texts of the bills, reports, hearings or prints in your library, you might have to know the Superintendent of Documents (SuDocs) number. This number begins with a "Y" and contains a colon. What is the SuDoc number of this hearing in Question 4?

Now, you will search the THOMAS website using the same public law as Question 1. THOMAS accesses legislative information on the Internet without a fee. Go to http://thomas.loc.gov. Take a few minutes to familiarize yourself with the site.

6. Locate the **Museum and Library Services Act**, Pub. L. No. 108-81 by first clicking on Public Laws, then the 108th Congress. Next, locate the correct public law. What is the bill number that passed into law? Hint: The abbreviation "H.R." proceeds the bill number if it originated in the House of Representatives or an "S." if it originated in the Senate.

    Instruction: Click on the bill number link and then on the following page, click on "ALL Congressional Actions."

7. Who was the main sponsor of the bill?

8. To which House committee was the bill referred?

9. What was the House Report number reported by the Committee on the Education and the Workforce on 2/25/2003? Cite it according to Rule 13.4 of *The Bluebook*.

10. Is the full text of the report available?

11. When did the President sign the bill?

ASSIGNMENT ELEVEN
FINDING AND CITING ADMINISTRATIVE MATERIALS
EXERCISE A

GOALS OF THIS ASSIGNMENT:
To acquaint you with finding federal regulations and administrative decisions in your library.
To familiarize you with the rules for citing regulations and administrative decisions in *The Bluebook: A Uniform System of Citation*, 18th ed.

CITATION RULES: You will need to read Rules 14.1-14.3 (including subsections) and refer to tables T.1, T.6, T.10 and T.12. Apply these rules as you determine the correct citation for each regulation and decision. All of the materials in this assignment are U.S. government documents and may be shelved in the government documents area of your library.

The first question requires you to find and cite a regulation in the C.F.R. Cite all federal rules and regulations to the C.F.R. by title, section, and year. Include the name of the regulation if it is commonly known by its name. **Example: 7 C.F.R. § 1902.6 (2004).**

1. Find and cite the most recent edition of the *Code of Federal Regulations*, section 4.1 of Title 42. Do not include the name of the regulation.

The next question requires you to find and cite a regulation in the daily *Federal Register*. Citations of regulations should give the commonly used name (if appropriate), the volume and page on which the regulation begins, and the exact date. When the *Federal Register* indicates where the rule will appear in the C.F.R., give that information in parentheses. **Example: 67 Fed. Reg. 49,599 (July 31, 2002) (to be codified at 38 C.F.R. pt. 20).**

2. Find the *Federal Register* for January 4, 2005 at p. 426 and cite the regulation correctly. Do not include the name of the regulation.

Next, you must find a proposed rule (that is, one that is not promulgated) in the *Federal Register* and cite it correctly. When citing proposed rules, follow the form for final rules (see above example), but also add the exact date it was proposed. **Example: 60 Fed. Reg. 3371 (proposed Jan. 17, 1995) (to be codified at 49 C.F.R. pt. 40).**

3. Find the *Federal Register* for January 10, 2005 at p. 1774 and cite it correctly. Do not include the name of the proposed regulation.

Now, find and cite an administrative decision or adjudication. When citing an administrative decision, cite by case name, report, and date - see Rule 14.3. The case name should only be the first-listed private party or subject-matter title. NOTE: If the case does not appear in an official agency reporter, then cite to a looseleaf service; see Rule 19 for details. **Example: *John Staurulakis, Inc.*, 4 F.C.C.R. 516 (1988).**

4. Find the administrative decision involving Jack in the Box in volume 339 of the *Decisions and Orders of the National Labor Relations Board*. You may need to seek assistance from your librarian to locate administrative decisions in your library. Provide the full citation of the case. Be sure to use abbreviations from Table T.6. 6 of *The Bluebook* when citing names of cases.

The *Federal Register*, the C.F.R., and many administrative decisions are online on WESTLAW and LEXIS. You can locate administrative materials on the Internet at http://www.nara.gov and http://www.access.gpo.gov .

GOALS OF THIS ASSIGNMENT:
To acquaint you with finding federal regulations and administrative decisions in your library.
To familiarize you with the rules for citing regulations and administrative decisions in *The Bluebook: A Uniform System of Citation*, 18th ed.

CITATION RULES: You will need to read Rules 14.1-14.3 (including subsections) and refer to tables T.1, T.6, T.10 and T.12. Apply these rules as you determine the correct citation for each regulation and decision. All of the materials in this assignment are U.S. government documents and may be shelved in the government documents area of your library.

The first question requires you to find and cite a regulation in the C.F.R. Cite all federal rules and regulations to the C.F.R. by title, section, and year. Include the name of the regulation if it is commonly known by its name. **Example: 7 C.F.R. § 1902.6 (2004).**

1. Find and cite the most recent edition of the *Code of Federal Regulations*, section 11.36 of Title 44. Do not include the name of the regulation.

The next question requires you to find and cite a regulation in the daily *Federal Register*. Citations of regulations should give the commonly used name (if appropriate), the volume and page on which the regulation begins, and the exact date. When the *Federal Register* indicates where the rule will appear in the C.F.R., give that information in parentheses.
Example: 67 Fed. Reg. 49,599 (July 31, 2002) (to be codified at 38 C.F.R. pt. 20).

2. Find the *Federal Register* for January 12, 2005 at p. 1995 and cite the regulation correctly. Do not include the name of the regulation.

Next, you must find a proposed rule (that is, one that is not promulgated) in the *Federal Register* and cite it correctly. When citing proposed rules, follow the form for final rules (see above example), but also add the exact date it was proposed. **Example: 60 Fed. Reg. 3371 (proposed Jan. 17, 1995) (to be codified at 49 C.F.R. pt. 40).**

3.   Find the *Federal Register* for January 6, 2005 at p. 1211 and cite it correctly. Do not include the name of the proposed regulation.

Now, find and cite an administrative decision or adjudication. When citing an administrative decision, cite by case name, report, and date - see Rule 14.3. The case name should only be the first-listed private party or subject-matter title. NOTE: If the case does not appear in an official agency reporter, then cite to a looseleaf service; see Rule 19 for details. **Example: *John Staurulakis, Inc.*, 4 F.C.C.R. 516 (1988).**

4.   Find the administrative decision involving Horizons Satellite in volume 19 of the *Federal Communications Commission Record*. You may need to seek assistance from your librarian to locate administrative decisions in your library. Provide the full citation of the case. Be sure to use abbreviations from Table T.6. 6 of *The Bluebook* when citing names of cases.

The *Federal Register*, the C.F.R., and many administrative decisions are online on WESTLAW and LEXIS. You can locate administrative materials on the Internet at http://www.nara.gov and http://www.access.gpo.gov .

ASSIGNMENT ELEVEN
FINDING AND CITING ADMINISTRATIVE MATERIALS
EXERCISE C

GOALS OF THIS ASSIGNMENT:
To acquaint you with finding federal regulations and administrative decisions in your library.
To familiarize you with the rules for citing regulations and administrative decisions in *The Bluebook: A Uniform System of Citation*, 18th ed.

CITATION RULES: You will need to read Rules 14.1-14.3 (including subsections) and refer to tables T.1, T.6, T.10 and T.12. Apply these rules as you determine the correct citation for each regulation and decision. All of the materials in this assignment are U.S. government documents and may be shelved in the Government Documents area of your library.

The first question requires you to find and cite a regulation in the C.F.R. Cite all federal rules and regulations to the C.F.R. by title, section, and year. Include the name of the regulation if it is commonly known by its name. **Example: 7 C.F.R. § 1902.6 (2004).**

1. Find and cite the most recent edition of the *Code of Federal Regulations*, section 153.460 of Title 46. Do not include the name of the regulation.

The next question requires you to find and cite a regulation in the daily *Federal Register*. Citations of regulations should give the commonly used name (if appropriate), the volume and page on which the regulation begins, and the exact date. When the *Federal Register* indicates where the rule will appear in the C.F.R., give that information in parentheses.
Example: 67 Fed. Reg. 49,599 (July 31, 2002) (to be codified at 38 C.F.R. pt. 20).

2. Find the *Federal Register* for January 11, 2005 at p. 1972 and cite the regulation correctly. Do not include the name of the regulation.

Next, you must find a proposed rule (that is, one that is not promulgated) in the *Federal Register* and cite it correctly. When citing proposed rules, follow the form for final rules (see above example), but also add the exact date it was proposed. **Example: 60 Fed. Reg. 3371 (proposed Jan. 17, 1995) (to be codified at 49 C.F.R. pt. 40).**

3.   Find the *Federal Register* for January 5, 2005 at p. 773 and cite it correctly. Do not include the name of the proposed regulation.

Now, find and cite an administrative decision or adjudication. When citing an administrative decision, cite by case name, report, and date - see Rule 14.3. The case name should only be the first-listed private party or subject-matter title. NOTE: If the case does not appear in an official agency reporter, then cite to a looseleaf service; see Rule 19 for details. **Example: *John Staurulakis, Inc.,* 4 F.C.C.R. 516 (1988).**

4.   Find the administrative decision involving the Westinghouse Electric Corporation in volume 1 of the *Interstate Commerce Commission Reports*, Second Series. You may need to seek assistance from your librarian to locate administrative decisions in your library. Provide the full citation of the case. Be sure to use abbreviations from Table T.6. 6 of *The Bluebook* when citing names of cases.

The *Federal Register*, the C.F.R., and many administrative decisions are online on WESTLAW and LEXIS. You can locate administrative materials on the Internet at http://www.nara.gov and http://www.access.gpo.gov .

ASSIGNMENT ELEVEN
FINDING AND CITING ADMINISTRATIVE MATERIALS
EXERCISE D

GOALS OF THIS ASSIGNMENT:
To acquaint you with finding federal regulations and administrative decisions in your library.
To familiarize you with the rules for citing regulations and administrative decisions in The Bluebook: A Uniform System of Citation, 18th ed.

CITATION RULES: You will need to read Rules 14.1-14.3 (including subsections) and refer to tables T.1, T.6, T.10 and T.12. Apply these rules as you determine the correct citation for each regulation and decision. All of the materials in this assignment are U.S. government documents and may be shelved in the government documents area of your library.

The first question requires you to find and cite a regulation in the C.F.R. Cite all federal rules and regulations to the C.F.R. by title, section, and year. Include the name of the regulation if it is commonly known by its name. **Example: 7 C.F.R. § 1902.6 (2004).**

1. Find and cite the most recent edition of the *Code of Federal Regulations*, section 192.513 of Title 49. Do not include the name of the regulation.

The next question requires you to find and cite a regulation in the daily *Federal Register*. Citations of regulations should give the commonly used name (if appropriate), the volume and page on which the regulation begins, and the exact date. When the *Federal Register* indicates where the rule will appear in the C.F.R., give that information in parentheses.
Example: 67 Fed. Reg. 49,599 (July 31, 2002) (to be codified at 38 C.F.R. pt. 20).

2. Find the *Federal Register* for January 3, 2005 at p. 144 and cite the regulation correctly. Do not include the name of the regulation.

Next, you must find a proposed rule (that is, one that is not promulgated) in the *Federal Register* and cite it correctly. When citing proposed rules, follow the form for final rules (see above example), but also add the exact date it was proposed. **Example: 60 Fed. Reg. 3371 (proposed Jan. 17, 1995) (to be codified at 49 C.F.R. pt. 40).**

3. Find the *Federal Register* for January 7, 2005 at p.1403 and cite it correctly. Do not include the name of the proposed regulation.

Now, find and cite an administrative decision or adjudication. When citing an administrative decision, cite by case name, report, and date - see Rule 14.3. The case name should only be the first-listed private party or subject-matter title. NOTE: If the case does not appear in an official agency reporter, then cite to a looseleaf service; see Rule 19 for details. **Example: *John Staurulakis, Inc.*, 4 F.C.C.R. 516 (1988).**

4. Find the administrative decision involving Dell Computers in volume 128 of the *Federal Trade Commission Decisions*. You may need to seek assistance from your librarian to locate administrative decisions in your library. Assume that the subsequent history of the case is unknown. Provide the full citation of the case. Be sure to use abbreviations from Table T.6.6 of *The Bluebook* when citing names of cases.

The *Federal Register*, the C.F.R., and many administrative decisions are online on WESTLAW and LEXIS. You can locate administrative materials on the Internet at http://www.nara.gov and http://www.access.gpo.gov .

ASSIGNMENT TWELVE
FEDERAL ADMINISTRATIVE RULES AND REGULATIONS
EXERCISE A

GOALS OF THIS ASSIGNMENT:
To develop your ability to find printed federal final regulations on a specific topic or issued pursuant to authority granted by a particular statute.
To give you experience in determining whether an agency has changed a regulation.
To search the C.F. R. and *List of Sections Affected* on the Internet.

To answer Questions 1-2, use the Index volume to the *Code of Federal Regulations* (any year), published by the Government Printing Office.
Note: The C.F.R. and *Federal Register* are also on LEXIS, WESTLAW, and on the Internet at: http://www.gpoaccess.gov/cfr/index.html.

1.   Using the Parallel Table of Authorities and Rules, labeled "Authorities," in the Index volume, state which title and part of the C.F.R. were adopted under the authority of **22 U.S.C. § 4137**, the code section you used in Assignment Nine. By using this table you can find regulations if you already have the U.S.C. citation.

2.   Now use the subject index in the same Index volume. Find and cite the regulations on gasoline and alternative fuel transportation programs.

Reshelve the Index volume.

3.   Find the text of the regulation part from the previous question. What is the statutory authority for the regulation part? State the **first** reference to the U.S.C. as printed in the C.F.R.

4.   Where did the first regulation from the part in Question 3 appear in the *Federal Register*? State the source note as printed in the C.F.R.

To update the C.F.R. use the slim pamphlet, *List of C.F.R. Sections Affected*. Use the *List of C.F.R. Sections Affected* to answer Questions 5 and 6.

5.   Using the *List of CFR Sections Affected*, June 2002, determine if any change occurred in 33 C.F.R. § 155.810. What is the status of that section?

6.   Where would you find this change in the 2001 *Federal Register*?

Use the Internet to answer Questions 7 and 8.

7.   Repeat Question 2 using the GPO website
      http://www.gpoaccess.gov/cfr/index.html.
      What search terms led you to the regulation? Hint: When performing search, use quotation marks around search terms to obtain best results.

8.   Repeat Question 5 using the GPO website
      http://www.gpoaccess.gov/lsa/browse.html.
      Did you find the same answer to Question 5?

ASSIGNMENT TWELVE
FEDERAL ADMINISTRATIVE RULES AND REGULATIONS
EXERCISE B

GOALS OF THIS ASSIGNMENT:
To develop your ability to find printed federal final regulations on a specific topic or issued pursuant to authority granted by a particular statute.
To give you experience in determining whether an agency has changed a regulation.
To search the C.F. R. and *List of Sections Affected* on the Internet.

To answer Questions 1-2, use the Index volume to the *Code of Federal Regulations* (any year), published by the Government Printing Office.
Note: The C.F.R. and *Federal Register* are also on LEXIS, WESTLAW, and on the Internet at: http://www.gpoaccess.gov/cfr/index.html.

1. Using the Parallel Table of Authorities and Rules, labeled "Authorities," in the Index volume, state which title and part of the C.F.R. were adopted under the authority of **29 U.S.C. § 2005**, the code section you used in Assignment Nine. By using this table you can find regulations if you already have the U.S.C. citation.

2. Now use the subject and agency index in the same Index volume. Find and cite the regulations on watermelon research and promotion

Reshelve the Index volume.

3. Find the text of the regulation part from the previous question. What is the statutory authority for the regulation part? State the source note to the U.S.C. as printed in the C.F.R.

4. Where did the first regulation from the part in Question 3 appear in the *Federal Register*? State the source note as printed in the C.F.R.

To update the C.F.R. use the slim pamphlet, *List of C.F.R. Sections Affected*. Use the *List of C.F.R. Sections Affected* to answer Questions 5 and 6.

5. Using the *List of CFR Sections Affected*, December 2003, determine if any change occurred in 11 C.F.R. § 105.2. What is the status of that section?

6. Where would you find this change in the 2003 *Federal Register*?

Use the Internet to answer Questions 7 and 8.

7. Repeat Question 2 using the GPO website http://www.gpoaccess.gov/cfr/index.html. What search terms led you to the regulation? Hint: When performing search, use quotation marks around search terms to obtain best results.

8. Repeat Question 5 using the GPO website http://www.gpoaccess.gov/lsa/index.html. Did you find the same answer to Question 5?

ASSIGNMENT TWELVE
FEDERAL ADMINISTRATIVE RULES AND REGULATIONS
EXERCISE C

GOALS OF THIS ASSIGNMENT:
To develop your ability to find printed federal final regulations on a specific topic or issued pursuant to authority granted by a particular statute.
To give you experience in determining whether an agency has changed a regulation.
To search the C.F.R. and *List of Sections Affected* on the Internet.

> **To answer Questions 1-2, use the Index volume to the *Code of Federal Regulations* (any year), published by the Government Printing Office.**
> **Note: The C.F.R. and *Federal Register* are also on LEXIS, WESTLAW, and on the Internet at: http://www.gpoaccess.gov/cfr/index.html.**

1. Using the Parallel Table of Authorities and Rules, labeled "Authorities," in the Index volume, state which title and part of the C.F.R. were adopted under the authority of **42 U.S.C. § 300g-3**, the code section you used in Assignment Nine. By using this table you can find regulations if you already have the U.S.C. citation.

2. Now use the subject and agency index in the same Index volume. Find and cite the regulations on standards for egg products.

    Reshelve the Index volume.

3. Find the text of the regulation part from the previous question. What is the statutory authority for the regulation part? State the **first listed** title and section to the U.S.C. as printed in the C.F.R.

4. Where did the first regulation from the part in Question 3 appear in the *Federal Register*? State the source note as printed in the C.F.R.

To update the C.F.R. use the slim pamphlet, *List of C.F.R. Sections Affected*. Use the *List of C.F.R. Sections Affected* to answer Questions 5 and 6.

5. Using the *List of CFR Sections Affected*, September 2004, determine if any change occurred in 47 C.F.R. § 87.151. What is the status of that section?

6. Where would you find this change in the 2004 *Federal Register*?

Use the Internet to answer Questions 7 and 8.

7. Repeat Question 2 using the GPO website http://www.gpoaccess.gov/cfr/index.html. What search terms led you to the regulation? Hint: When performing search, use quotation marks around search terms to obtain best results.

8. Repeat Question 5 using the GPO website http://www.gpoaccess.gov/lsa/browse.html Did you find the same answer to Question 5?

ASSIGNMENT TWELVE
FEDERAL ADMINISTRATIVE RULES AND REGULATIONS
EXERCISE D

GOALS OF THIS ASSIGNMENT:
To develop your ability to find printed federal final regulations on a specific topic or issued pursuant to authority granted by a particular statute.
To give you experience in determining whether an agency has changed a regulation.
To search the C.F. R. and *List of Sections Affected* on the Internet.

> **To answer Questions 1-2, use the Index volume to the *Code of Federal Regulations* (any year), published by the Government Printing Office.**
> **Note: The C.F.R. and *Federal Register* are also located on LEXIS, WESTLAW, and on the Internet at:** http://www.gpoaccess.gov/cfr/index.html.

1. Using the Parallel Table of Authorities and Rules, labeled "Authorities," in the Index volume, state which title and parts of the C.F.R. were adopted under the authority of **20 U.S.C. § 107a**, a related code section to the one you used in Assignment Nine. By using this table you can find regulations if you already have the U.S.C. citation.

2. Now use the subject and agency index in the same Index volume. Find and cite the regulations on funeral industry practices.

Reshelve the Index volume.

3. Find the text of the regulation part from the previous question. What is the statutory authority for the regulation part? State the **first** source note to the U.S.C. as printed in the C.F.R.

4. Where did the regulation from the part in Question 3 appear in the *Federal Register*? State the source note as printed in the C.F.R.

To update the C.F.R. use the slim pamphlet, *List of C.F.R. Sections Affected*. Use the *List of C.F.R. Sections Affected* to answer Questions 5 and 6.

5.   Using the *List of CFR Sections Affected*, March 2003, determine if any change occurred in 47 C.F.R. § 1.1103. What is the status of that section?

6.   Where would you find this change in the 2002 *Federal Register*?

Use the Internet to answer Questions 7 and 8.

7.   Repeat Question 2 using the GPO website
      http://www.gpoaccess.gov/cfr/index.html.
      What search terms led you to the regulation? Hint: When performing search, use quotation marks around search terms to obtain best results.

8.   Repeat Question 5 using the GPO website
      http://www.gpoaccess.gov/lsa/browse.html.
      Did you find the same answer to Question 5?

ASSIGNMENT THIRTEEN
REVIEW--FINDING STATUTES AND REGULATIONS
EXERCISE A

GOAL OF THIS ASSIGNMENT:
Require you to use statutes and regulations to solve research problems.

In this assignment, you will review statutory and regulatory research. You will find statutory law, legislative history, and regulations.

Ms. Smith is the Law Library Director of large academic law library and has a staff of exempt and nonexempt staff. One of Ms. Smith's long-time exempt staff members, Amy, has just given birth to Emma. Amy wants to apply for a leave under the Family and Medical Leave Act and understands that the leave will be unpaid. However, Amy is worried that the unpaid leave will affect her exempt status as a Library Associate I.

You are a clerk in your university attorney's office. The Law Library Director contacts the university attorney for advice and he turns the research over to you. You decide to begin with the federal annotated code since the question involves a federal law.

1. Use the Index in U.S.C.A. to determine the appropriate code section. Look up the act and answer the following questions.
    a. What is the correct citation to the code section that answers the question? Note: Use Rule 12 and table T.1 in *The Bluebook*.

    b. Will Amy lose her exempt status if she goes on unpaid family leave?

2. Examine the section. What is the Public Law number of the 1993 act?

3. Under Library References, what is the West topic and key number on Civil Rights?

4. Under Historical and Statutory Notes, find references to the legislative history of the 1993 act. Obtain the citation to U.S.C.C.A.N. On what page of the 1993 U.S.C.C.A.N. does the legislative history begin?

5. Under Library References, where would you find regulations on employees' entitlement to leave in the C.F.R.?

6. Next, examine the Notes of Decisions. Find a 1998 Circuit Court of Appeals case on the attempt by an employee to seek leave under FMLA for the adoption of two children of his brother in the Philippines. What is the name of the case?
    Hint: Make sure you check the pocket part.

Reshelve U.S.C.A. and find U.S.C.C.A.N.

7. Examine the legislative history in the 1993 U.S.C.C.A.N. from Question 4. Which Senate report is reprinted in U.S.C.C.A.N.?
    Hint: Look in the Legislative History pages of the 1993 U.C.C.C.A.N.

Reshelve U.S.C.C.A.N. and find C.F.R.

8. Look up the regulation from Question 5 in the C.F.R. How many workweeks of leave during any twelve-month period is an eligible employee limited to under the FMLA?

ASSIGNMENT THIRTEEN
REVIEW--FINDING STATUTES AND REGULATIONS
EXERCISE B

GOAL OF THIS ASSIGNMENT:
Require you to use statutes and regulations to solve research problems.

In this assignment, you will review statutory and regulatory research. You will find statutory law, legislative history, and regulations.

Mr. Jones is the Law Library Director of large academic law library that has a sizeable print and audio visual collection. One law librarian, Judy, wants to make ten copies of soothing commercial music to be housed in the reserve collection. Judy feels that the music will ease the students' stress level. The Law Library Director feels that this type of copying in a library is an infringement of copyright law.

You are a clerk in your university attorney's office. The Law Library Director contacts the university attorney for advice and he turns the research over to you. You decide to begin with the federal annotated code since the question involves a federal law.

1. Use the Index in U.S.C.A. to determine the appropriate code section. Look up the act and answer the following questions.

    a. What is the correct citation to the code section? Note: Use Rule 12 and table T.1 in *The Bluebook*.

    b. Can the librarian make ten copies of commercial music for the reserve collection?

2. Examine the section. What is the Public Law number of the Oct. 28, 1998 amendment? Hint: Make sure you check the pocket part.

3. Under Library References, what is the West topic and key number on the topic?

4.   Under Historical and Statutory Notes, find references to the legislative history of the 1992 act. Obtain the citation to U.S.C.C.A.N. On what page of the 1992 U.S.C.C.A.N. does the legislative history begin?

5.   Under Library References, where would you find regulations on copyright warnings in the C.F.R.?

6.   Next, examine the Notes of Decisions. Find a 1990 case involving New York's Standardized Testing Act. What is the name of the case?

Reshelve U.S.C.A. and find U.S.C.C.A.N.

7.   Examine the legislative history in the 1992 U.S.C.C.A.N. from Question 4. Which House report is reprinted in U.S.C.C.A.N.?
      Hint: Look in the Legislative History pages of the 1992 U.C.C.C.A.N.

Reshelve U.S.C.C.A.N. and find C.F.R.

8.   Look up the regulation from Question 5 in the C.F.R. What is the minimum size (in points) for the printing of a "Display Warning of Copyright"?

GOAL OF THIS ASSIGNMENT:
Require you to use statutes and regulations to solve research problems.

In this assignment, you will review statutory and regulatory research. You will find statutory law, legislative history, and regulations.

Mr. Richards is a Law Library Director of large academic law library. In the Law Library, several energetic librarians, including Mary, want to market the library using familiar slogans. One of Mary's ideas is to use the American Express trademark and attach the slogan "Don't Leave Home Without It" to the library circulation card. Although this idea would be noncommercial use of the trademarked slogan, the Law Library Director is concerned that the American Express credit card company may have a problem with the library using their famous trademark and slogan.

You are a clerk in your university attorney's office. The Law Library Director contacts the university attorney for advice and he turns the research over to you. You decide to begin with the federal annotated code since the question involves a federal law.

1. Use the Index in U.S.C.A. to determine the appropriate code section. Look up the act and answer the following questions.

    a. What is the correct citation to the code section that answered the question? Note: Use Rule 12 and table T.1in *The Bluebook*.

    b. Is noncommercial use of a famous mark or slogan actionable under the federal trademark laws?

2. Examine the section. What is the Public Law number of the 1996 amendment?

3. Under Library References, what is the West topic and key number on the topic?

4. Under Historical and Statutory Notes, find references to the legislative history of the 1996 act. Obtain the citation to U.S.C.C.A.N. On what page of the 1995 U.S.C.C.A.N. does the legislative history begin?

5. Under Library References, where would you find regulations on false designations of origin and description of trademarks in the C.F.R.?

6. Next, examine the Notes of Decisions. First, find the topic "Colors." Find a 1989 Court of Appeals case involving the use of basic colors in its logo. What is the name of the case?

Reshelve U.S.C.A. and find U.S.C.C.A.N.

7. Examine the legislative history in the 1995 U.S.C.C.A.N. from Question 4. Which House report is reprinted in U.S.C.C.A.N.?
    Hint: Look in the Legislative History pages of the 1995 U.C.C.C.A.N.

Reshelve U.S.C.C.A.N. and find C.F.R.

8. Look up the regulation from Question 5 in the C.F.R. They specifically cover which two precious metals in this regulation?

ASSIGNMENT THIRTEEN
REVIEW--FINDING STATUTES AND REGULATIONS
EXERCISE D

GOAL OF THIS ASSIGNMENT:
<u>Require you to use statutes and regulations to solve research problems.</u>

In this assignment, you will review statutory and regulatory research. You will find statutory law, legislative history, and regulations.

Ms. Holland is the Law Library Director of large academic law library in a quaint college town. The College of Law has housed the law library in a beautiful historic property dating from the turn of the century. One of the law school's wealthy donors will contribute several million dollars if the law library's property is on the National Register of Historic Places. The Law Library Director asks who is authorized to expand the National Register of Historic Places to include the law library.

You are a clerk in your university attorney's office. The Law Library Director contacts the university attorney for advice and he turns the research over to you. You decide to begin with the federal annotated code since the question involves a federal law.

1. Use the Index in U.S.C.A. to determine the appropriate code section. Look up the act and answer the following questions.

    a. What is the correct citation to the code section that answered the question? Note: Use Rule 12 and table T.1 in *The Bluebook*.

    b. Who authorizes the expansion of the National Register of Historic Places?

2. Examine the section. What is the Public Law number of the original 1966 act?

3. Under Library References, what are the West topic and key numbers under United States?

4.   Under Historical and Statutory Notes, find references to the legislative history of the 1976 act. Obtain the citation to U.S.C.C.A.N. On what page of the 1976 U.S.C.C.A.N. does the legislative history begin?

5.   Under Library References, where would you find regulations on the protection of archaeological resources for the Office of Secretary of the Interior in the C.F.R.?

6.   Next, examine the Notes of Decisions. First, find the topic "Site or object." Next, find a 1997 case stating that a tree may qualify for the National Register of Historic Places. What is the name of the case?

Reshelve U.S.C.A. and find U.S.C.C.A.N.

7.   Examine the legislative history in the 1976 U.S.C.C.A.N. from Question 4. Which House report is reprinted in U.S.C.C.A.N.?
      Hint: Look in the Legislative History pages of the 1976 U.C.C.C.A.N.

Reshelve U.S.C.C.A.N. and find C.F.R.

8.   Look up the regulation from Question 5 in the C.F.R. Provisions of what 1979 Act are implemented by the regulations in this section?

ASSIGNMENT FOURTEEN
SECONDARY AUTHORITY
EXERCISE A

GOALS OF THIS ASSIGNMENT:
To familiarize you with one of the two major legal encyclopedias and your state legal encyclopedia.
To introduce you to the legal periodical indexes and how to cite legal periodical articles.
To show you how to find treatises in your library.
To introduce you to looseleaf services.

Answer Questions 1-2 using *American Jurisprudence 2d.*

1. Provide the complete citation to the section that discusses the need for a new trial when jurors use an atlas during deliberations. Use *Bluebook* form, Rule 15.8(a).

2. Look up the section. This section indicates it is generally harmless error for jurors to consult a dictionary or atlas. State the name of the Illinois case that is cited for this proposition.

3. Does your state have a legal encyclopedia? If so, state the title of the encyclopedia.

   To answer Questions 4 and 5, use either *LegalTrac, Current Law Index,* or *Index to Legal Periodicals.* Refer to Rule 16 and table T.13. Look at the actual articles to cite them.

4. Provide the complete citation to a 2001 article on the structure of judicial opinions.

5. State the citation of the 2000 article on the case *Baker v. State* that appeared in the ABA Journal. Note: This magazine is not consecutively paged, so follow Rule 16.4.

6.   If your law library holds this issue, where is this periodical in your library? Either provide a row number or call number. Indicate if your library has the article online.

You should use your library's online catalog to answer questions 7 and 8.

7.   Find the 2003 hornbook on the law of modern payment systems by Frederick H. Miller in your library. Cite it according to Rule 15.

8.   Find the 2004 nutshell on white collar crime by Ellen S. Podgor. Provide the call number or location of the book in your library.

Answer questions 9 and 10 using *ABA/BNA Lawyers' Manual On Professional Conduct* in print or online. Hint for online searchers: Browse the website for the Ethics Opinions area, use the ABA Ethics Opinions link, and type your search into the search box at the top of the page.

9.   State the citation to the 2004 ABA Formal Ethics Opinion that obligates a lawyer to report professional misconduct by a lawyer not engaged in the practice of law. Cite it according to Rule 12.8.6.

10.   Browse the text of the ethics opinion from question 9. Under what Model Rule number does the lawyer's obligation to report professional misconduct by a lawyer not engaged in the practice of law accrue? Cite the answer according to Rule 12.8.6.

ASSIGNMENT FOURTEEN
SECONDARY AUTHORITY
EXERCISE B

GOALS OF THIS ASSIGNMENT:
To familiarize you with the use one of the two major legal encyclopedias and your state legal encyclopedia.
To introduce you to the legal periodical indexes and how to cite legal periodical articles.
To show you how to find treatises in your library.
To introduce you to looseleaf services.

Answer Questions 1 and 2 using *American Jurisprudence 2d.*

1.   Provide the complete citation of the section that discusses if a lieutenant governor in her capacity as acting governor can grant pardons. Use *Bluebook* form, Rule 15.8(a).

2.   Look up the section. State the name of the North Carolina case that discusses the validity of a pardon given by a lieutenant governor as acting governor.

3.   Does your state have a legal encyclopedia? If so, state the title of the encyclopedia.

To answer Questions 4 and 5 use either *LegalTrac, Current Law Index, or Index to Legal Periodicals.* Refer to Rule 16 and table T.13. Look at the actual articles to cite them.

4.   Provide the citation to the 2001 article on Joseph McCarthy as a law student.

5.   State the citation of the October 2003 article on the case *Lawrence v. Texas* that appeared in the ABA Journal. Note: This journal is not consecutively paged, so follow Rule 16.4.

6.   If your law library holds this issue, where is this periodical in your library? Either provide a row number or call number. Indicate if your library has the article online.

      You should use your library's online catalog to answer questions 7 and 8.

7.   Find the 2003 hornbook on land use planning by Julian Juergensmeyer. Cite it according to Rule 15.

8.   Find the 2003 nutshell on national security and military law by Charles Shanor and L. Lynn Hogue. Provide the call number or location of the book in your library.

      Answer questions 9 and 10 using *ABA/BNA Lawyers' Manual On Professional Conduct* in print or online. Hint for online searchers: Browse the website for the Ethics Opinions area, use the ABA Ethics Opinions link, and type your search into the search box at the top of the page. You may also use the Master Index link found on the website to search for your answer.

9.   State the citation to the 2003 Formal Ethics Opinion that articulates a lawyer's duty to report rule violations by another lawyer who may suffer a disability. Cite it according to Rule 12.8.6.

10.   Browse the text of the ethics opinion from question 9. State the ABA Model Rule that is broken if a lawyer continues representation of a client while the attorney is suffering from a disability. Cite the answer according to Rule 12.8.6.

ASSIGNMENT FOURTEEN
SECONDARY AUTHORITY
EXERCISE C

GOALS OF THIS ASSIGNMENT:
To familiarize you with one of the two major legal encyclopedias and your state legal encyclopedia.
To introduce you to the legal periodical indexes and how to cite legal periodical articles.
To show you how to find treatises in your library.
To introduce you to looseleaf services.

Answer Questions 1 and 2 using *American Jurisprudence 2d.*

1.   Provide the complete citation of the sections that discuss photographing an accused murderer's teeth as an invasion of privacy. Use *Bluebook* form, Rule 15.8(a).

2.   Look up the section. State the name of an Illinois case that held that there was no improper invasion of an accused murderer's privacy when the police took a photograph of his teeth for use in evidence.

3.   Does your state have a legal encyclopedia? If so, state the title of the encyclopedia.

To answer Questions 4 and 5, use either *LegalTrac, Current Law Index, or Index to Legal Periodicals.* **Refer to Rule 16 and table T.13. Look at the actual articles to cite them.**

4.   Provide the citation to a 2001 article on Medicaid expansion and the limits of incremental reform.

5.   State the citation of the 2004 article written about the case *Rosner v. United States* that appeared in the ABA Journal. Note: This journal is not consecutively paged, so follow Rule 16.4.

6.   If your law library holds this issue, where is the legal periodical in your library? Either provide a row number or call number. Indicate if your library has the article online.

You should use your library's online catalog to answer questions 7 and 8.

7.   Find the 2002 hornbook on the law of securities regulation by Thomas Hazen. Cite according to Rule 15.

8.   Find the 2003 nutshell on family law by Harry Krause. Provide the call number or location in your library.

Answer questions 9 and 10 using the CCH *Standard Federal Tax Reporter* in print or online. Hints for online searchers using the CCH Tax Research Network: Choose the Federal tab, scroll to the bottom of the screen to the Topical Indexes section, and choose *Standard Federal Income Tax Reporter*.

9.   State the paragraph number that explains the discharge of all or part of a student loan without income recognition to the debtor.

10.   State the paragraph number that defines the useful life of a sawmill equipment.

ASSIGNMENT FOURTEEN
SECONDARY AUTHORITY
EXERCISE D

GOALS OF THIS ASSIGNMENT:
To familiarize you with one of the two major legal encyclopedias and your state legal encyclopedia.
To introduce you to the legal periodical indexes and how to cite legal periodical articles.
To show you how to find treatises in your library.
To introduce you to looseleaf services.

Answer Questions 1 and 2 using *American Jurisprudence 2d.*

1.   Provide the complete citation to the section that discusses the exemption of appliances from claims of creditors. Use *Bluebook* form, Rule 15.8(a).

2.   Look up the section. State the name of the Texas case that addresses freezers as exempt from claims of creditors.

3.   Does your state have a legal encyclopedia?   If so, state the title of the encyclopedia.

To answer Questions 4 and 5, use either *LegalTrac, Current Law Index, or Index to Legal Periodicals*. Refer to Rule 16 and table T.13. Look at the actual articles to cite them.

4.   Provide the complete citation to a 2001 article on law student loans.

5.   State the citation of the 1998 article written about the case *United States v. Scheffer* that appeared in the ABA Journal.   Note: This journal is not consecutively paged, so follow Rule 16.4.

6.　　If your law library holds this issue, where is this periodical in your library? Either provide a row number or call number. Indicate if your library has the article online.

You should use your library's online catalog to answer questions 7 and 8.

7.　　Find the 2003 hornbook on intellectual property by Roger Schechter in your library. Cite it according to Rule 15.

8.　　Find the 2000 nutshell on contracts by Claude Rohwer. Provide the call number or location in your library.

Answer questions 9 and 10 using the CCH _Standard Federal Tax Reporter_ in print or online. Hints for online searchers using the CCH Tax Research Network: Choose the Federal tab, scroll to the bottom of the screen to the Topical Indexes section, and choose _Standard Federal Income Tax Reporter_.

9.　　State the paragraph number that discusses personal exemptions for the birth of a dependent.

10.　　State the paragraph number that explains whether lottery ticket winnings can be counted in the gross income of the lottery winner.

ASSIGNMENT FIFTEEN
REVIEW--FINDING SECONDARY AUTHORITY
EXERCISE A

GOALS OF THIS ASSIGNMENT:
To review the use of sources of secondary authority.
To emphasize how the various publications cross reference users to other materials.

You are a clerk in a small general practice law firm. One day Harry makes an appointment to talk to Kathy, an attorney in your firm, about his divorce. Harry's biggest concern is how to divide his lottery jackpot from the previous year. Harry feels that his big winnings will be one of the most contested issues in his divorce.

Since Kathy has never dealt with the division of lottery proceeds in a divorce proceeding, she asks you to find out some general information to counsel her client when he visits her office. Kathy wants to read some background information before she delves into cases.

1.   Into what broad areas of the law does this question fall?

2.   Using your online catalog, find a treatise in your library on divorce. List the author, title, and date of publication.

3.   Try the periodical indexes, such as LegalTrac or *Index to Legal Periodicals & Books*, either in print or online. Find a 1993 article that discusses lottery prizes in divorce and property issues. The article appeared in the Suffolk University Law Review. Find the article in your library and cite it according to Rule 16 of *The Bluebook*.

4. Another good source of secondary authority is A.L.R. Use the A.L.R. Index and find an A.L.R.5th annotation published in 2004 on Harry's issue. **Hint: Be sure to check pocket parts for latest updates.** Look up the annotation and provide the citation according to Rule 16.6.6.

5. Now examine the beginning of the A.L.R. annotation. Note the different types of cross references to other publications and related annotations. What is the reference to Am. Jur. 2d where you would find a discussion of this issue?

6. *American Jurisprudence 2d* may also provide background information on an area of unfamiliar law. Find the topic and section of Am. Jur. 2d from Question 5 and answer the following question. Without a statute or a reservation by the court, can a court modify a permanent alimony decree?

GOALS OF THIS ASSIGNMENT:
To review the use of sources of secondary authority.
To emphasize how the various publications cross reference users to other materials.

You are a clerk in a small general practice law firm in Michigan. One day David makes an appointment to talk to Jennifer, an attorney in your firm, about an injury he sustained when he slipped on a parking lot at a neighborhood hotel. On one snowy Saturday evening David exited the hotel and fell in the hotel's snow packed parking lot. David felt that the owner of the hotel should be liable for his hospital bill and time off from work.

Since Jennifer has never dealt with a slip and fall case, she asks you to find out some general information to counsel her client when he visits her office. Jennifer wants to read some background information before she delves into case law.

1. Into what broad areas of the law does this question fall?

2. Using your online catalog, find a treatise in your library on negligence. List the author, title, and date of publication.

3. Try the periodical indexes, such as LegalTrac or *Index to Legal Periodicals & Books*, either in print or online. Find a 1985 article discussing "slip and fall" liability of hotels. The article appeared in the Santa Clara Law Review. Find the article in your library and cite it according to Rule 16 of *The Bluebook*.

4. Another good source of secondary authority is A.L.R. Use the A.L.R. Index and find an A.L.R.5th annotation published in 1999 on David's issue. **Hint: Be sure to check pocket parts for latest updates.** Look up the annotation and provide the citation according to Rule 16.6.6.

5. Now examine the beginning of the A.L.R. annotation. Note the different types of cross references to other publications and related annotations. What is the reference to Am. Jur. 2d where you would find a discussion under the topic Premises Liability?

6. *American Jurisprudence 2d* may also provide background information on an area of unfamiliar law. Find the topic and section 699 of Am. Jur. 2d from Question 5 and answer the following question.   To avoid liability, does the owner of the premises generally owe a duty to pedestrians to keep the public sidewalk free from snow and ice?

ASSIGNMENT FIFTEEN
REVIEW--FINDING SECONDARY AUTHORITY
EXERCISE C

GOALS OF THIS ASSIGNMENT:
To review the use of sources of secondary authority.
To emphasize how the various publications cross reference users to other materials.

You are a clerk in a small general practice law firm. One day Joe makes an appointment to talk to Carol, an attorney in your firm, about being searched on a cruise ship because of the odor of marijuana emanating from his clothes. Joe was cruising in the islands when an officer approached him and escorted him into a room where the officer conducted a warrantless strip search.

Since Carol has never dealt with a warrantless search based on the odor of marijuana, she asks you to find out some general information to counsel her client when he visits her office. The attorney wants to read some background information before she delves into case law.

1.   Into what broad areas of the law does this question fall?

2.   Using your online catalog, find a treatise in your library on search and seizure. List the author, title, and date of publication.

3.   Try the periodical indexes, such as LegalTrac or *Index to Legal Periodicals & Books*, either in print or online. Find a 1980 article discussing search and seizure on the high seas. The article appeared in the Loyola Law Review. Find the article in your library and cite it according to Rule 16 of *The Bluebook*.

4.   Another good source of secondary authority is A.L.R. Use the A.L.R. Index and find an A.L.R.5th annotation published in 2004 on Joe's issue. **Hint: You will be looking for an entry under state cases. Be sure to check pocket parts for latest updates.** Look up the annotation and provide the citation according to Rule 16.6.6.

5.   Now examine the beginning of the A.L.R. annotation. Note the different types of cross references to other publications and related annotations. What is the reference to Am. Jur. 2d where you would find a discussion under the topic Searches and Seizures?

6.   *American Jurisprudence 2d* may also provide background information on an area of unfamiliar law. Find the topic and section 10 of Am. Jur. 2d from Question 5 and answer the following question. Are all searches and seizures prohibited by the Fourth Amendment?

GOALS OF THIS ASSIGNMENT:
To review the use of sources of secondary authority.
To emphasize how the various publications cross reference users to other materials.

You are a clerk in a small general practice law firm. One day Jack makes an appointment to talk to Suzanne, an attorney in your firm, about being accused of unauthorized practice of law. Jack is a realtor and was present at his client's real estate closing when the clients started asking him for legal advice. Since he always worked with attorneys, he answered their questions. When the officials at the State Bar heard of Jack's behavior, the bar sued Jack for unauthorized practice of law.

Since Suzanne has never dealt with unauthorized practice of law, she asks you to find out some general information to counsel her client when he visits her office. Suzanne wants to read some background information before she delves into case law.

1. Into what broad areas of the law does this question fall?

2. Using your online catalog, find a treatise in your library on unauthorized practice of law. List the author, title, and date of publication.

3. Try the periodical indexes, such as LegalTrac or *Index to Legal Periodicals & Books*, either in print or online. Find a 1992 article analyzing the role of the broker and the purchaser. The article appeared in the Brigham Young University Law Review. Find the article in your library and cite it according to Rule 16 of *The Bluebook*.

4.   Another good source of secondary authority is A.L.R. Use the A.L.R. Index and find an A.L.R.5th annotation published in 2004 on Jack's issue. **Hint: Be sure to check pocket parts for latest updates.** Look up the annotation and provide the citation according to Rule 16.6.6.

5.   Now examine the beginning of the A.L.R. annotation. Note the different types of cross references to other publications and related annotations. What is the reference to Am. Jur. 2d where you would find a discussion of the issue?

6.   *American Jurisprudence 2d* may also provide background information on an area of unfamiliar law. Find the topic and section of Am. Jur. 2d from Question 5 and answer the following question. Does the practice of law include preparing instruments and contracts by which legal rights are secured?

ASSIGNMENT SIXTEEN
WESTLAW – PART ONE

GOALS OF THIS ASSIGNMENT:
To formulate effective search strategies in researching case law.
To introduce you to terms and connectors searching, natural language searching, field searching, FIND, KeyCite, and Table of Authorities.

Use **WESTLAW** at <u>http://lawschool.westlaw.com</u>. Refer to Rule 18.1 and its subsections on Commercial Electronic Databases in *The Bluebook*.

Answer Question 1 before you sign on WESTLAW.

1. Assume you want to find state cases on the following fact situation. You are an attorney representing a baseball coach who was assaulted by a volunteer manager and assistant coaches of the opposing team. He wants to know if the league is responsible for his injuries. Formulate your query by choosing terms and connectors to specify the relationship between the terms. Use the WESTLAW materials. Write your query using terms and connectors.

2. **Sign on WESTLAW to complete the assignment.** You want to find an Illinois state case that deals with this fact situation. Use the **Directory** link at the top of the page. You can use the Database Wizard or browse the Directory. What is the appropriate database identifier for this research?

3. Retrieve a 2000 Supreme Court of Illinois opinion concerning the query from Question 1. What is the complete citation of the case?

4. Natural Language searching on WESTLAW allows you to search using standard English instead of terms and connectors. To change to Natural Language, select the **Edit Search** link. Now click on **Natural Language**. Use the same fact situation from Question 1 and type your search. Did you find the same Supreme Court of Illinois case from 2000?

KeyCite is West's citation service that enables you to determine if your case is good law and to find other sources that have cited your case. When viewing a particular case, you will see a History link and a Citing References link. You may also see case history indicators in the document header. If the case has negative history, you will see either a red or yellow case status flag. If the case has some history that is not necessarily negative, a blue H will appear in the header. A green C indicates that the case has citing references, but no direct or negative indirect history.

5. Now, KeyCite the same opinion from Questions 3 and 4 by clicking on the flag in the document header. You should be using the **History** link. What is the name of the 2002 Illinois case that "declined to extend by?"

6. To view the sources that have cited your case, click on **Citing References.** What is the name of the August 2002 Illinois Appellate case that mentions your case? Hint: Look at depth of treatment indicators for "mentioned."

7. Click on **Limit KeyCite Display**. You can limit citing references by headnote, locate term, jurisdiction, date, document type, or depth of treatment. Click on document type and locate law review articles. How many articles are listed?

8. You can limit KeyCite to display only the cases that from a specific jurisdiction. Limit KeyCite to the cases from Missouri. Make sure you check "Other courts" under **Document Type** tab. What is the name of the 2002 Missouri case?

Cancel the limits by clicking on the Cancel Limits link. If necessary, return to the spilt-page view by clicking on the Spilt-Page View icon.

9. Select the **Table of Authorities** by clicking on the **Table of Authorities** link. Table of Authorities lists the cases cited **in** your case and enables you to see if any of the cases your case relied on have significant negative history. Click on the **Table of Authorities** link for the *Hills* case decided in 2000. How many cases were cited in your case?

186

10.   Next you will use the **Find** service. You can find a document by citation or title. Select the **Find** link from the toolbar. Retrieve the case at 118 S. Ct. 1. State the name of the case.

11.   You can also find a document by its title. Click on **Find**, then on the link **Find a Case by Party Name**. Click on **State Courts** and select **Connecticut** from the drop down box. Locate a Connecticut case titled *Jackson v. Johnson* dated Dec. 16, 1986. What are the volume and page number of the citation in the regional reporter?

12.   To begin a new search in a database, go to the Westlaw Directory by selecting the **Directory** link from the toolbar. Select **Georgia state** cases. You want to locate all of the cases involving the Georgia attorney Deborah A. Edwards. To restrict a search to the attorney field, click on the **Fields** link. What is the field abbreviation to locate an attorney?

13.   Type in the attorney's name in the attorney field box. Locate cases involving Deborah A. Edwards. How many cases are displayed? Remember, using quotations will limit searches to an exact name phrase.

14.   To display a specific case in the citation list, click on the name of the case in the list. Click on the case decided November 29, 1990. State the plaintiff's **first** and **last** name.

15. To begin a new search in a different database, select the **Directory** link. In the **Search these databases** box in the Database Directory frame on the left, type in the federal database **CTA7** and click **GO**. To view a detailed description of a database, click on the Scope icon **"i."** What is in the CTA7 database?

16. KeySearch is a research tool that helps you find cases and secondary sources within a specific area of the law. KeySearch guides you through the selection of terms from a classification system based on the West Key Number System and then uses the key numbers and their underlying concepts to formulate a query for you. Click **KeySearch** on the toolbar. Locate cases with headnotes from South Carolina on nursing home license revocation. Click on Health - Nursing Homes - License revocation. Under **Choose a source**, make sure **Cases with West Headnotes** is selected. Then select **South Carolina State** cases from the drop down box. Make sure you check the box before this selection. What is the name of a 1988 case?

The **Research Trail** automatically creates a record of tasks you complete during a research session. You may want to view the trail, deliver the trail via email, download it, or print it. Remember to sign off WESTLAW by clicking **Sign Off**.

GOALS OF THIS ASSIGNMENT:
To give you practice at formulating effective search strategies for researching statutes, regulations, secondary materials, and non-legal materials.
To introduce you to FIND, terms and connectors searching, natural language searching, and field searching.

Use WESTLAW at http://lawschool.westlaw.com. **Refer to Rule 18.1 and its subsections on Commercial Electronic Databases in** *The Bluebook.*

1. When you know a statute's citation, FIND is the easiest method for retrieving the statute. You need not enter a database; you can simply click on **Find** and you are in **Find a Document**. You want to find Ind. Code Ann. § 3-3-3-3. Type **In. St. 3-3-3-3** in the **Find this Document by Citation** box. What is the topic of this section?

2. To leave your found document and return to the database directory, select the **Directory** link on the toolbar. The **Find a Database Wizard** will walk you through the process of selecting a database that meets your research needs. The **Find a Database Wizard** is available from the Directory page. Locate the database for the Mo. Ann. Stat. What is the database identifier? Click on the Scope icon **"i"** to see the database identifier.

3. Click on **MO-ST-ANN**. Locate a statute designating the date for Arbor Day. State the citation according to *Bluebook* Rule 18.1.2.

4. To begin a new search in a new database, select the **Directory** link from the toolbar. Type **TN-ST**, the Tennessee unannotated statutes database, in the **Search these databases** box and click **GO**. You can limit your search to a specific field. To see which fields are available in this database choose the Terms and Connectors search method and click the **Scope i icon**. Then click on the **Searching and Fields** link. Scroll down toward the bottom of the scope document. You will see a list of the fields and their definitions. What material is included in the caption of a statute?

Click twice on your browser's Back button to go back to the TN-ST database query page.

5.   Now, use the caption field to search. Locate a statute from Tennessee on rules on wagering by using the caption field. State the statute citation.

6.   In statutory documents, you can view consecutive statutes. Click on the link in the lower right-hand corner of the screen that says **Tools.** Then click on **Documents in Sequence**. WESTLAW automatically displays the next statute in sequence after your original statute. You can move either forward by clicking on the **Right** arrow at the bottom or backward by clicking on the **Left** arrow at the bottom of the screen. Click on the **Left** arrow to get back to your original statute from Question 5. Click on the **Left** arrow twice to get to the statute that precedes your original statute by two. State the section number for that statute and the title of that section.

7.   We now want to conduct a search in the U.S.C. Access the U.S.C. database by clicking on the **Directory** link at the top of the page. Type **USC** in the **Search these databases** box and click **GO**. Locate the federal statute establishing West Point.

8. To retrieve federal regulations, access the Code of Federal Regulations (CFR) database by clicking on the **Directory**. Type **CFR** in the **Search these databases** box and click **GO**. Locate the regulation discussing salmon in the Columbia River Basin.

9. Any final regulations published in the *Federal Register* that were issued after the latest C.F.R. database revision will be displayed automatically. Are there any new regulations from your answer to Question 8? If so, list the citations.

10. You can search either the full text of legal periodicals on WESTLAW or the various indexes to legal periodicals. The *Legal Resource Index* database (LRI) includes all material covered in the *Current Law Index*. Access the LRI database by clicking the **Directory** link at the top of the page. Type **LRI** in the **Search these databases** and click **GO**. Locate articles on defective tire rims. State the citation of the article that appeared in the 1991 issue of *Trial*.

11. Natural Language searching on WESTLAW allows you to search using standard English instead of terms and connectors. To change to Natural Language, select the **Edit Search** link in the left frame. Now click on **Natural Language**. Use the same fact situation from Question 10 and type your search. Did you find the same 1991 law review article from *Trial*?

12.   Next, click on **Directory**, then **Business & News**. Click on **Business & News: Complete Alphabetical List** then **Databases beginning with B**. Is the *Baltimore Sun* included?

13.   Click on **Baltimore Sun (MD) (BALTSUN)**. Locate a 2002 article in the Baltimore Sun written by Liz Atwood that discusses an ice cream mixer. What is the exact date of the article?

14.   The West Legal Directory database (WLD) contains information on attorneys, courts, judges, and judicial clerkships. To access the West Legal Directory, click the   **Directory** link, then **Directories, Reference** then **West Legal Directories** and finally **West Legal Directory (WLD)**. Locate Stephen Kelly in Peoria, Illinois by using the template. What is the name of his firm?

The **Research Trail** automatically creates a record of tasks you complete during a research session. You may want to view the trail, deliver the trail via email, download it, or print it. Remember to sign off WESTLAW by clicking **Sign Off**.

ASSIGNMENT EIGHTEEN
LEXIS -- PART ONE

GOALS OF THIS ASSIGNMENT:
To give you practice at subject searches in case law and other sources.
To introduce you to Shepard's, Search Advisor, and Get a Document.

Answer Question 1 before you begin your research on LEXIS. Refer to *Understanding Lexis.com* **or other reference material. Refer to Rule 18.1 and its subsections on Commercial Electronic Databases in** *The Bluebook.*

Assume that you are looking for state cases on the following fact situation. You are an attorney representing the driver of an automobile who was involved in a nighttime collision at an intersection where the traffic signals were not working due to a power outage. She wants to know what duty of care is required at an intersection with an inoperative traffic light.

1. Write out the search using terms and choosing connectors.

Sign on to LEXIS on the Internet at http://www.lexisnexis.com/lawschool and click on the **Research System** tab.

2. First, click on **Research System**, then **Search tab - Sources**. Find the relevant Court of Appeals of Washington case decided in 2001 and reported in the *Pacific Reporter*. Click on **States Legal - U.S. > Washington > WA State Cases, Combined**. Run your search. State the full citation of the case using the *Bluebook* citation format in Rule 10.

3. If you click on Custom viewing, how would you view the case?

4. What do you click on to view the document quickly to see if it is on point?

5. The **FOCUS** feature conducts a search within your results to target specific words within your search results. Is the case, *Whitchurch v. McBride*, cited in your case? Type your search in the FOCUS Terms box located on the FOCUS bar.

6.   On what page of the *Pacific Reporter* is this case discussed? Look for the page number preceded by **.

7.   The Natural Language feature on LEXIS allows you to search in plain English, rather than using connectors. Click on the **Search** tab. Choose from **Recently Used Sources - WA State Cases, Combined**. To change to Natural Language, click on the **Natural Language** button. Use the same fact situation from Question 1 and type your search. Did you find the same 2001 Court of Appeals of Washington case? Make sure you locate the case published in P.3d.

8.   In your case, you will notice core terms. What are core terms?

9.   You already know that Shepard's offers full treatment and history analysis needed to verify the status of a case. Additionally, Shepard's provides you with a list of documents related to the issue that you are researching. Shepardize this 2001 Washington case by clicking on the **Shepard's signal** at the top of the case. What does the signal mean?

10.   Examine the Shepard's display. How do you get specific citations that meet your research needs?

11.   Click on **Custom** at the top of the screen. Click the box for dissenting opinions (**Dissenting Op.**). State the name of the case whose dissenting opinion cites your case.

12.   Click on the case from Question 11. Did this case also involve an intersection collision?

13.   You can also Shepardize by clicking on the **Shepard's** tab. Shepardize 196 F.3d 900. What does the Shepard's symbol indicate?

14.   From the citations listed in the results obtained in Question 13, what is the name of the opinion that has criticized your case?

15.   You can also begin your research by clicking on the **Search Advisor** tab. Find family law cases on nonparental custody statutes. Click on **Family Law**, click on **Child Custody**, click on **Awards**, then choose **State Family Law Cases** from the **Select Jurisdiction** drop down menu of the case tab. Type your search request as a terms and connectors search. How many cases are on the topic?

16.   You can also start with a particular citation to a case, a statute, or a law review article. Click on **Get a Document** - then click on the **Citation** sub-tab. You are looking for the full text of a case, so click the **Full Text** button. Type 643 N.W.2d 359. What is the name of the case?

17.   You can also get a case by its name. Click on **Get a Document** tab. Click on the **Party Name** sub-tab. Type Zadvydas and Davis in the windows. Then click **US Courts of Appeals** and select **5th Circuit** from the drop down menu. Click on **Search**. What is the F.3d citation of this case?

18.   Lastly, you can retrieve a case by its docket number. Click on **Get a Document**, then the **Docket Number** sub-tab. Type 98-8384 and click on **US Supreme Court**. Click on **Search**. What is the name of the case?

Sign off LEXIS.

ASSIGNMENT NINETEEN
LEXIS -- PART TWO

GOAL OF THIS ASSIGNMENT:
To give you practice at formulating effective search strategies for researching statutes, regulations, and secondary materials on LEXIS.

> This assignment was designed to be completed using LEXIS at http://www.lexisnexis.com/lawschool. Refer to Rule 18.1 and its subsections on Commercial Electronic Databases in *The Bluebook*. Logon to LEXIS and select the Research System tab.

1. When you know a statute's citation and want to retrieve its text, you should use **Get a Document**. You need not enter a database, you can simply type a citation into **Get a Document**. Click on the **Get a Document** tab, click on the **Citation** sub-tab. You want to find Mont. Code Ann. § 26-1-803. Type the citation. What is the topic of the section?

2. **Book Browse** allows you to view preceding and succeeding code sections of the statute without constructing another search request. Click on **Book Browse** located at the top of the screen. Using the citation from Question 1, what is the section number of the previous section?

3. Next locate a statute on medical power of attorney in the Texas database. To leave your found document and return to the sources screen, select the **Search** tab to be in **Sources - Look for a Source - Legal** . Click on **States Legal - U.S.** Next click on **Texas**, then **Statutes & Regulations**. Finally click on **TX-Texas Statutes and Codes Annotated by LexisNexis**. What is the citation of the statute that indicates the form for the medical power of attorney? Type your search terms. State the citation according to *The Bluebook*.

4. How many treatises and analytical materials are listed?

5. To begin a new search in a different database, click on the **Search** tab. Under **Look for a Source,** click on the **Find a Source** tab. In the box, type **United States Code Service**. In the **Find a Source Results**, click on **United States Code Service - Titles 1 through 50**. Search for the federal law that mandates that the Director of the Patent and Trademark Office maintain a library of scientific and other works and periodicals, both foreign and domestic.

6. Next use the Minnesota database to search the Minnesota Statutes.. Click **Search**. Under **Look for a Source**, click on the **Find a Source** tab. In the box, type **Minnesota Statutes**. In the **Find a Source Results**, select **MN - LexisNexis Minnesota Annotated Statutes**. Locate the statute that addresses the immunity from liability of a school bus driver under the Good Samaritan laws.

7. To retrieve federal regulations, access the Code of Federal Regulations (C.F.R.) database by first clicking on **Search,** then **Look for a Source**, then **Find a Source**. In the search box, type **CFR**. Select **CFR - Code of Federal Regulations** from the **Find a Source Results**. Locate the regulation that states financial assistance is the purpose of the early intervention program for infants and toddlers with disabilities.

8. Any final regulations published in the *Federal Register* that were issued after the latest C.F.R. database revision will be displayed automatically. How current is the section?

9. Use the C.F.R. section from Question 7and use the FOCUS feature to conduct another search within a document. Type **minority** in the **FOCUS Terms box.** Does this term appear in this C.F.R. section?

10. Now go to the *Arkansas Democrat-Gazette* newspaper file. Click on **Search,** then **Look for a Source**, then **Find a Source.** In the search box, type **Arkansas Democrat-Gazette** and select it from the **Find a Source Results**. Run a search using Document Segments by using the Terms and Connectors search. Segments are divisions or sections within a document. Segments can help to narrow your research by retrieving documents with relevant information in certain areas of the documents. Look for an article on inductees into the Boys and Girls Club Hall of Fame by Raschke. Byline is one of the segments. In the **Enter Search Terms** box, enter the first part of your search. Under the **Restrict by Segment**, add the byline segment. In the first pull-down box, select your segment **BYLINE**. In the next box, type **Raschke**. Click on the **Add** button. What is the date of the article?

11. For this question, you will be looking for a law review article. Click on **Search,** then **Look for a Source**, then **Find a Source.** In the search box, type **Law Reviews**. Select **US Law Reviews and Journals, Combined** from the **Find a Source Results**. Find an article that appeared in 1999 on parallel litigation that was published in the *Baylor Law Review*. Who is the author of the article?

12. Natural Language searching on LEXIS allows you to search using standard English instead of terms and connectors. To change to Natural Language, click on **Natural Language**. Use the same fact situation from Question 11 and type your search. Did you find the same 1999 article from the *Baylor Law Review*?

13. Martindale-Hubbell Law Directory is available on LEXIS. Click on **Search,** then **Look for a Source**, then **Find a Source.** In the search box, type **CA Listings Martindale-Hubbell Law Directory**. Locate California attorney Mark Theodore. Remember to switch back to Terms and Connectors searching. Use the **NAME** segment. Where did Mark Theodore attend law school?

Sign off LEXIS.